Go the Way Your Blood Beats: On Truth, Bisexuality and Desire

Go the Way Your Blood Beats: On Truth, Bisexuality and Desire

MICHAEL AMHERST

Published by Repeater Books
An imprint of Watkins Media Ltd

Unit 11, Shepperton House
89-93 Shepperton Road
London
N1 3DF
UK
www.repeaterbooks.com
A Repeater Books paperback original 2018
2

Distributed in the United States by Random House, Inc., New York.

Cover design: Johnny Bull
Typography and typesetting: Stuart Davies
Typefaces: Palatino

ISBN: 9781910924716
Ebook ISBN: 9781910924730

Printed and bound in the United Kingdom

Contents

Ah, but a man's reach should exceed his grasp,
Or what's a heaven for?

– Robert Browning, "Andrea del Sarto"

Best advice I ever got was an old friend of mine, a black friend, who said you have to go the way your blood beats. If you don't live the only life you have, you won't live some other life, you won't live any life at all. That's the only advice you can give anybody. And it's not advice, it's an observation.

– James Baldwin interviewed by Richard Goldstein, *The Village Voice*, June 26, 1984.

On the one hand, I'm aware that I have no right to this story. What is it I can tell? But on the other, I'm the only one who can tell it. If that story is simply and truly how I related to you, how I miss you, what it means to be myself, to live within my head, heart and hands and how you made me see and live a little more clearly – that story can only ever be told by me. So, as always, this is not a story about you but a story about me. For that I'm sorry. But it could only ever be this way.

Sexuality is about much more than whom we have sex with. Sexuality isn't always about sex, but sex is always about sexuality.

Sexuality can be integral to our sense of self and the way we perceive the world. So much so that we can presume others' experience of their sexuality must be the same as our own. I am anxious not to do so here. However, a claim to the unknowability of sexuality – a desire for an openness that allows us all to act on our desire for an *individual*, without fear of our previous desires being reassessed or rewritten – seems to me a positive. It is a call for something beyond tolerance. It is not predicated on a belief that we are all bisexual, but that any of us *might* be. Such a stance realises that love is rarely expected. It is a belief in James Baldwin's observation as to the universal value of all people and that:

> Love is the lightening of life. Love is where you find it. Your maturity, I think, is signalled by the depth of the extent to which you can accept the dangers and the power and the beauty of love.[1]

In 2013, British Olympic diver Tom Daley released a YouTube video[2] in which he announced that he was in a relationship with a man. He said he was attracted to both men and women, and simply wanted to make the fact of his relationship clear. The UK press termed this a "coming out", with *Pink News*, the UK's largest LGBT news agency, using the headline "Tom Daley comes out as gay".[3] This he had demonstrably not done.

Two weeks later, Daley appeared on the ITV panel show *Celebrity Juice*. In their opening exchange, the host of the show bluntly asked Daley, "So you're gay now? You're a gay man now?" To which Daley laughed awkwardly, before replying yes.

I, like anyone who does not fit neatly into the either/or of gay and straight, find Daley's momentary hesitation and awkwardness familiar. Do I accept "gay" as the general term for all of those outside of heterosexuality? Do I want to invite further questions about my private life? Do I – in front of a large TV audience, in a light-hearted, jovial environment – disrupt the rhythm by giving a lengthy and detailed explanation of my sexuality? Do I say no, I'm bisexual – even though that word doesn't accurately describe how I feel either? Do I take issue, even when I *am* a man in a relationship with a man so, to all intents and purposes, could be meaningfully described as gay, right now? Or do I simply make the quick calculation that it's not worth bothering with in this moment, and say, as Tom Daley did, "Yes"?

These words, "gay" and "bi", are not neutral; they are

not without their problems. Many people described as bisexual find the term problematic because it reinforces a sense that attraction is a binary of either/or; also, that to be "truly" bisexual one must demonstrate an exact balancing of attraction between men and women. One study[4], which interviewed Canadian students about bisexual identification, found they believed anything other than an exact split of attraction and sexual activity suggested a preference that revealed an individual's "true sexuality". Not only does this make the parameters for anything outside of gay and straight impossibly high, it also mandates a degree of investigation and reporting of an individual's desire that is intolerable.

My experience, and that of many others commonly termed bisexual, is that desire waxes and wanes between the sexes. Even within that, I can meet someone who contravenes my usual sense of what I desire. It also raises questions about what society means by desire – how each of us may desire different things from different people and maybe even from either sex. An awareness of such fluidity can also be unsettling. The demand to identify as either/or can leave one in a state of constant flux.

Social attitudes towards bisexuality are starkly different, none more so than the different responses to men and women. The "taint of homosexuality" often means that even a single same-sex encounter can be levelled against a man as proof that he is "really" gay. A man who has debased himself by not conforming to the masculine paradigm is forever other. On the other hand, a woman is often perceived to be performing same-sex activity for the titillation of a male subject. Our society's intrinsic misogyny means her sexuality, her very agency, can only be seen through this prism. She demeans herself, not through same-sex desire, but only when she dismisses men altogether.

If I must have a word, I prefer the word queer. It is an acknowledgement of my exclusion from exclusive heterosexuality, without claiming a certainty as to where my sexuality sits amongst straight, bisexual or gay. It is an admission, while at the same time a refusal to engage in the policing of my past relationships in search of my "true" orientation.

When undergraduates at my college demanded "S" was added to LGBTQ, for "straight", my tutor asked why it was necessary because Q can include everything. This definition of queer – as a broad, inclusive term for those deemed in some way outside of the norm – is one I can rally behind. I like that it may include heterosexuals who deny otherness, or have heterosexual sex perceived as deviant by the mainstream. This seems important. Not only does it break down the barriers of "otherness", it also suggests a future that is genuinely inclusive.

When Maggie Nelson[5] prickles at straight, white men describing their work as queer, asking, "Do you have to own everything?", I feel differently. I'm dubious about straight, white men describing only their work as queer, but for the same men to describe *themselves* as queer seems, to me, a victory. It rejects a distinction, and any underlying value judgements, about straight sex. Queer is a denial of the terms of the question, a denial of its validity. If you're asked "Are you gay?", "Are you bi?", "Are you straight?", queer gives no ground. It's an inclusive term for any who perceive the unreality of binary sexuality.

It's a refusal to speak. Not out of shame. But it's a refusal to speak, to confirm what I don't know, can't know; a refusal because it doesn't and shouldn't matter; and a refusal because, chiefly, it is none of your business.

The day after his *Celebrity Juice* appearance, the national newspapers reported that – two weeks after saying he was attracted to men and women – "already" Daley had confessed that really he was gay. *Really* he was gay. *The Daily Star*[6] subheading read: "Tom Daley has revealed that he is 'a gay man' – not bisexual as he first said". *The Independent* wrote: "Tom Daley is gay – not bisexual as he said on YouTube", with the subheading, "The Olympic diving medallist confirms that he no longer fancies women". Most vociferous was *Pink News*[7], which ran the headline, "Tom Daley: I'm definitely gay not bisexual", and in the body of the article, "Explaining why he initially suggested he was bisexual, Daley said: 'I came out on YouTube as I wanted to say what I wanted to say without anyone twisting it.'" But these headlines were a complete fabrication. At no stage did Daley discuss his attraction to women or use the terms gay or bisexual. His response was not an "explanation" as to "why he initially suggested he was bisexual", it was a response to a question about why he used YouTube to announce his relationship.

Eighteen months later, Daley told *The Guardian*[8] in an interview that he remained attracted to men and women. When asked if he regarded himself as bisexual, he replied, "I don't put a particular label on any of it because right now I'm in a relationship with a guy, but I still have sexual feelings towards girls." He then went on to mention that his partner, Dustin Lance Black, also felt opposite-sex attraction, although he identified as gay. But this time there was no media storm. Even *The Guardian* chose the headline "Tom Daley: 'I always knew I was attracted to guys'," lest anyone should be in any doubt which box to put Daley in.

Yet, returning to Daley's original video message: he never labels himself as gay or bisexual; he does not describe himself as in "a gay relationship"; he does not use the phrase "coming out". Instead, he simply makes it clear that he wants to be honest about his current relationship, does not want to be misquoted and, perhaps most significantly, does not want to be labelled by other people. The newspaper reports were fictions, misquoting Daley or quoting him out of context, all to satisfy a narrative that demanded he identify as gay.

Our right to define ourselves – as we are, in our infinite variety – as opposed to how others see us, is the fight of our lives. It was Baldwin's fight, against labels or identities that he found reductive of his human experience and a denial of the human dignity afforded to others. It is a fight for the recognition of our universal, human value.

> I was only fighting for safety, or for money at first. Then I fought to make you look at me. Because I was not born to be what someone said I was. I was not born to be defined by someone else, but by myself, and myself only.[9]

The notion of identity as something shared as opposed to personal is relatively new. In his 2016 BBC Reith Lectures, Kwame Anthony Appiah[10] gave the example of Rosamond in George Eliot's *Middlemarch* "almost losing the sense of her identity" on discovering that the man she loves is devoted to someone else. Such identity is utterly personal, Appiah argues, while what we think of as identity today – nationality, race, religion, sexuality – is composed of characteristics shared with many others: it is social. However, as his lectures argue, these traits are often constructed as a means of excluding as well as including. By constructing a shared sense of who we are, we codify the traits we deem undesirable or different from ourselves.

While I appreciate an anxiety that, in refusing to identify, individuals disown solidarity with others – a suspicion that we are guilty of our own form of homophobia – modern identities are not only shared socially, but can also be imposed. There can be an *imperative* to label and identify, one that forces an identity upon an individual that they have not chosen themselves. Such an act results from several different forms of presumption, failing to describe the fullness of an individual's lived reality.

Following years of speculation, in 2014 Olympic swimmer Ian Thorpe told Michael Parkinson[11] he was gay. This was at odds with denials he had issued in the past, including in his autobiography, *This Is Me*. Parts of the press were unremitting in both their criticism and their smugness that they had been right all along. But what does it even mean to be "right" in such a case? What does it mean "to know"?

Much of the speculation about Thorpe has been written by straight journalists with nothing to lose but everything to gain by filling column inches. There is something deeply homophobic about a culture that has long persecuted queer people, now demanding that we account for ourselves in a time and manner that satisfies the very people who have nothing to lose. Such a demand continues to treat us differently, while claiming to do so as an act of acceptance. Even as Thorpe acknowledges the relief and freedom he has felt since he gave the interview, he evidently did have something to lose, unlike his persecutors, telling Parkinson: "I guess I thought of everything I'd want in my life, a family, things like that. I was so young, I was trying to be everything for everyone and not having the confidence to just be myself."

Thorpe's anxieties about telling his parents of his battles with depression have an implicit equivalence with the anxieties and potential for loss in disclosing a non-normative sexuality:[12]

> I know how Mum will react; she'll cry and ask me why I didn't tell her and then she'll tell me how proud she is that I've finally talked about it. Dad is different. I'm not sure how he'll react. I know it'll take time for him to come to terms with it and how it fits in with his religious beliefs. I hope it does, because family means a lot to me. He once said that he felt he'd lost me as a son [when Thorpe was fifteen and competing on the world stage]. I hope, in my honesty, he'll feel as though he's gained me back.

I feel it shouldn't be controversial to suggest that acceptance of being queer can involve loss. Yet, I fear that we may be so caught up in a desire to project the positivity of a lived gay experience that this cannot be said. The structures that impose heteronormative expectations upon everyone within our society are our lived reality. We cannot deny this, nor should we. Thorpe alludes to this when he writes that "family means a lot to me" and he does not know how his father will react to his depression and "how it fits in with his religious beliefs."

I understand him and recognise this in my own experience. There is a conflict between the reasoning that can dismiss aspects of my parents' values and faith, which for a time discriminated against my same-sex desire, while at the same time acknowledging the emotional reality of being their child, desiring their love and acceptance. Similarly, there may be many ways for same-sex couples to have families and raise children. But I cannot deny the flood of love and wonder I feel seeing my sister's children and recognising in them the face and expressions of our late father. Yes – queer lives are rich and diverse and present other means of living, loving and raising children. But nor should it mean a denial of the feelings of loss for a life that cannot be lived.

A study in the *Journal of Bisexuality*[13] examined the phenomenon of those who initially come out as bisexual while knowing themselves to be gay. The author, Nicholas Guittar, found participants showed no fear of LGBQ identities, so much as a desire "to hold onto heteronormative conventions". Their misidentifying as bisexual was not so much out of internalised homophobia as internalised heteronormativity – a desire not to breach normative expectations. These expectations can be exterior, familial pressures or they can be internal, personal expectations. Either way, these pressures are real.

Yet, what Guittar found is that, far from coming out as bisexual alleviating the perceived social "disappointment" of friends and loved ones, each of those who misidentified as bisexual found themselves under a new pressure. Participants were told "it is a phase", "you better choose a sex", "I just wanted you to choose", "you can't be both. It just doesn't work... So, at some point you're going to have to pick one."

The results describe the difference between a public and a private sexuality in which, "public identities do not always align with private sexualities". It seems fair to suggest that such a difference is caused by a combination of social homophobia and what the study acknowledges as internalised heteronormativity. But Baldwin would argue that the point is moot: the idea of a public sexuality is a demand only placed on those outside of the normative. A true liberation would heed his call that we all deserve privacy, to live our lives without fear of scrutiny, as well as persecution.

The report concludes that claims of bisexuality as a transitional identity reinforce harmful stereotypes that hurt bisexuals and further a sense that it is "not a true sexual identity". In addition, the fact that some gay men and women have used bisexual as a transitional identity results in some of them presuming that this is always the case for others too.

The cliché of "bi now, gay later" is founded on several, unproven presumptions around sexuality. In an otherwise honest and generous piece by Owen Jones in *The Guardian*, I found myself arguing vociferously with a single line. When describing prejudice amongst gay men, Jones wrote, "they may start by coming out as bisexual (fuelling a sense of 'bi now, gay later', much to the annoyance of genuine bisexuals), hoping that having one foot in the straight camp might preserve a sense of normality."[14]

By saying "they may start by coming out as bisexual",

Jones maintains a narrative around sexuality as a journey with an end point. In his example, it is presumed that an earlier claim of bisexuality by a gay man or woman is always untrue – the only genuine sexuality is the final one. It is the destination. This furthers the sense that sexuality is an objective truth ("genuine bisexuals"); ergo, if you start by coming out as bisexual but later describe yourself as gay then you cannot have been genuine before. This problem is exacerbated by the language of "coming out" – a public revelation of a fixed truth, denied up until that point.

Jones' claim makes the presumption – also widely accepted – that anyone whose sexuality changes in later life has somehow been living a lie. Such an individual has only acknowledged the "truth", the "reality" of her sexuality later. This isn't to dismiss the testimony of those for whom that is exactly their experience. (Although, psychoanalysis teaches us to be aware of narratives that neatly redefine our past experience by present expediencies.) However, to simplistically apply that reading to all individuals who move from a heterosexual relationship to a homosexual one, or vice versa, maintains the fallacy that sexuality is a rigid, objective fact to be revealed. Besides denying the truth of someone's lived experience, we also dismiss their past relationships, and possibly any children from that relationship, as part of an earlier false-life.

George Michael, for example, called Kathy Yeung a "bona fide girlfriend" and never denied the fact of his earlier bisexuality.[15] He told *GQ* in 2004 that if he weren't with his then-partner he'd have sex with women. However, he identified as gay, dissecting his own, personal distinctions between identity and desire: "I would never be able to have a relationship with a woman because I'd feel like a fake. I regard sexuality as being about who you pair off with, and I wouldn't pair off with a woman and stay with her. Emotionally, I'm definitely a gay man."

It is all too easy for bisexuality to be erased when in a long-term relationship. At this point the confusion or fluidity of earlier seems moot. An individual is presumed to have reconciled to whichever gender they are in a relationship with now. This is coupled with a presumption that any previous relationship with the other gender was merely a phase, now left behind. This is to mistake a settled life and a stable relationship for an abandonment of bisexuality.

As we go through life, we make choices and form attachments that invest our lives with meaning. Yet it can also be increasingly hard to shift from a life we already know. Therefore, bisexuality is sometimes seen as mere youthful experimentation. But this is to mistake public expediency for interior knowledge. Whether you are in a heterosexual marriage and governor of your children's school or in a same-sex relationship and holiday with other gay couples, if your circle has become almost exclusively gay or almost exclusively straight, it can be difficult to meet someone outside of that circle, coupled with the potential risk of rejection. The artificial divisions between ways of life can make it harder to fulfil those other parts of ourselves as we age and have more to lose. Potentially, the greater inclusivity of gay people in mainstream communities, along with acceptance of a greater number of ways to live, mean that this is changing.

If you are attracted to both sexes and, quite probably, to differing degrees and to different people at different times, then there may be less sense of sexuality as either fixed or located in a sex as opposed to an individual. So, while sexuality may be a place of fixed certainty for some, it is not so for all. It can be a form of radical confusion. Yet, language around sexuality is infused with a sense of the genuine, the real and the true. When society insists on sexuality as always either/or, how are you to satisfy popular discourse? To know, or say, which of these attractions is "true" or most true?

The belief that sexuality is always a static, unchanging brute fact results in suspicion and discrimination, as opposed to curiosity, openness and acceptance.

Far from being, as some critics of bisexuality claim, an easier middle ground, the above study shows that those who fail to voice an either/or sexuality of gay or straight are often chided until they do. Guittar also found that as bisexuality involves same-sex attraction, it is seen by many as simply synonymous with gay.

I wonder whether the study ignores the possibility that by claiming a bisexual identity the candidates were making a claim for less exceptionalism and a greater degree of privacy. This, Guittar notes, is afforded to the heteronormative mainstream. The decision to disclose a bisexual identity "turned out to be based on false perceptions of what an individual's family or friends would be willing to accept. In the end, family and friends often pushed the individual to one end of the spectrum." Not only did they demand a sexuality that accords with contemporary understanding of sexuality as binary, they also mandated a sexuality that appeared more concrete than the potential fluidity of bisexuality. This may have something to do with a rigid understanding of sexuality that sees same-sex desire as distinct and separate. As Appiah observes with all forms of identity, the validation we seek in a shared sense of self is also predicated on excluding those whose commonality we seek to disown. We want a categorical sense of *them* as different from *us*.

Our language of sexuality is infused with suspicion, perhaps a symptom of its origins, as observed by Michel Foucault, in the confessional.[16] Gay or bisexual celebrities "confess" or "own up"; they "reveal" themselves or will "finally admit the truth". This was evident in the reporting of Thorpe, who was said to have "finally admitted" his sexuality. The reporting on Daley also supports Foucault's theory of systems of power that prescribe rather than describe experience, with journalists clamouring to identify Daley using words at odds with his own.

Discrimination against same-sex attraction and the

resulting shame have given rise to a language in which homosexuality is always perceived to go hand-in-hand with denial. This leads to an invidious behaviour in which society can call out both an individual's perceived homosexuality and their denial in an apparent display of its tolerance, a flexing of its liberal muscle. But this can also be viewed as a subtle form of intolerance – for if sexuality truly does not matter, why do we feel the obligation to call it out? It is also an act of presumed psychological and intellectual superiority over the object, and a presumption of almost constant and universal bad faith. Nothing is ever as it seems – instead, it is indicative of repression. Such a view is reductive of an individual's lived experience, and it presumes that the shame associated with homosexual desire runs so deep that a combination of either the desire or the shame is as far as we ever need to go in understanding an individual's actions.

Following Daley's video statement, Dom Joly wrote in *The Independent*: "I don't think that it came as much of a surprise to anyone, I certainly got a strong feeling when I met him that there was probably not going to be a Mrs Daley." One wonders why this needed saying. For a start, nothing Daley said at the time, nor since, has denied his attraction to women. Joly's statement is therefore grossly presumptuous. But many people, like Joly, feel a need to demonstrate that they are *in the know*. Yet, what is it they are claiming to know?

Joly went on: "He left his legions of girl fans a little bit of hope by saying that: 'I still fancy girls, obviously…'

This didn't seem to be too obvious to me. Whatever, I hope he got the reaction he hoped for and is happy in his life." Notice that "whatever" doing all the work! Joly says Daley's claim "didn't seem too obvious" to him, as though his intuition bears repeating and carries the validity of truth. These extracts make a claim of knowledge: that Joly has superior insight into the truth of Daley's desire, one that is more accurate than Daley's own account and understanding of himself. Yet, Joly at once tries to mask the arrogance of his position, so he chucks in a "whatever" to show he doesn't really care — save for the fact he obviously cares enough to have written a column about it for a national newspaper, to take the money and to make his doubts about Daley's sincerity public. Yet, despite the "whatever", despite the attempt to seem casual and not that bothered, the fact remains that Joly is calling Daley a liar.

This is policing of heterosexuality. As a married man with kids, who hasn't had to negotiate the fraught issue of societal homophobia, why does Daley's sexuality concern or interest Joly in the slightest? I ask again: what does it mean "to know"? And what is this knowledge based on?

Thorpe regularly commented, both prior to coming out and after, that much of the media speculation was rooted in the fact that he did not match up to the expectation of a straight sportsman. It is hard not to sense that such speculation is rooted in subtle forms of prejudice. More often than not, such "knowledge" is predicated on age-old stereotypes. For both men and women, it can be an inflection of the voice, a bearing, the odd mannerism. In Thorpe's case, it was his interest in culture and fashion, as though such an interest cannot be universal, but must be deemed suspicious. Such judgements are predicated on adherence to gender roles, as much as anything else.

If queer people let this go, if those of us who care about a society rooted in universal human dignity rather than cheap division let this go, if we argue that these acts of presumption and speculation do not matter because neither Daley nor Thorpe are straight, then we cede ground that is rooted in homophobia. For if Joly and others truly believe there is nothing wrong with being gay or queer, then why the need for virtue-signalling? Why the need to be acknowledged as sufficiently right-on that they could discern such facts, sometimes before the subjects themselves? Ultimately, if no one really cared then no one would feel the need to speculate, to place the imperative on Daley, Thorpe and others to identify both publicly and in a manner that accords with their own presumptions. For every one of those men and women who conform to a popular presumption of homosexuality, there are those who are straight but have their identity challenged for not appearing sufficiently so; just as there are those queer people told, "But I'd never have guessed." We should ask ourselves whether such statements are grounded in grace and love, or tinged with discrimination and a presumption about an individual's ability to successfully "other".

Of course, everyone makes presumptions; we all resort to lazy thinking. The difference is when we take our lazy thoughts for fact; worse still, facts to proclaim to others.

You were always much braver than I was. Like the night you were out with a friend, and two guys stopped you to ask for directions. You took out your phone and showed them on the map, said it wasn't far, and even asked if they'd like you to show them the way. Then you and your friend turned and left them, and when you were a little way down the street, one of them yelled after you: "Are you guys fags?" You turned, gave them the middle finger, and yelled: "You know what? Yes!"

Gay-bashing is an act of violent presumption. It presumes a knowledge about someone, then presumes to know what it means. Then that this meaning demands a violent response. Ultimately, it presumes a superiority based on those acts of presumption. But all presumptions about an individual's sexuality are acts of violence. They are presumptions about us, and presumptions as to what those things mean.

I reject the idea that we owe the world a compromised version of ourselves. Nelson puts it well when she talks of refusing "to engage with terms or forums that feel more like a compromise or distortion than an unbidden expression."

Generally, breaking into someone's locked desk and then rifling through their diary is regarded as an immoral thing to do. Taking what one has found there and reporting it to the world-at-large is a grave invasion of privacy. Reading only one page yet making assumptions about the individual, that you then broadcast, is not only an invasion of privacy but a denial of the other's agency: you place the individual in an invidious position whereby they can either accept the limited distortion you have sent out into the world, or deny it but only by breaching their privacy further, by opening up the diary and allowing the world to read all of what is written there. Yet for some reason, making such presumptions without even going to the trouble of breaking into the desk is seen as acceptable.

Such presumption denies us agency – to both be ourselves and to describe our experience for ourselves. This is my fight: to define myself and not accept the distortions of others. But in a way, this is still the same fight – because the presumption as to who I am and what it means is rooted in the same presumption that makes our world unsafe; the presumption that we are other, the presumption that yells: "Are you guys fags?"

Baldwin argued that homosexuality is universal. Or at least, that the distinction detracts from our universal humanity. "There's nothing in me that is not in everybody else, and nothing in everybody else that is not in me. We're trapped in language, of course. But 'homosexual' is not a noun." He describes the breakdown of sexuality into two categories as an artificial division: "Men will be sleeping with each other when the trumpet sounds. It's only this infantile culture which has made such a big deal of it."

In one of his final interviews, Baldwin tells Richard Goldstein that the word "gay" always rubbed him up the wrong way; he didn't apply it to himself, in part because he didn't know what was meant by it. Above all, Baldwin emphasises the personal in relation to sexuality and that – it being personal – should also make it private. Not hidden, but private. This doesn't mean a lack of responsibility towards gay people or "that phenomenon we call gay" because in this, as with so much else, Baldwin felt called to be a witness. Yet, in *Giovanni's Room*, he "made a public announcement that we're private, if you see what I mean."

Throughout the interview, Baldwin repeatedly calls attention to his lack of belief in the categories of sexuality. Besides questioning "gay" he also says that the only word he had was "homosexual" and this did not seem to describe his experience. He says if it is any part of speech then it might be a verb. He refers to "so-called" straight people and explicitly to sexual *preference* rather than identity. Goldstein struggles to comprehend, leading to a somewhat snarky final exchange:

BALDWIN: I loved a few people and they loved me. It had nothing to do with these labels. Of course, the world has all kinds of words for us. But that's the world's problem.

GOLDSTEIN: Is it problematic for you, the idea of having sex only with other people who are identified as gay?

BALDWIN: Well, you see, my life has not been like that at all. The people who were my lovers were never, well, the word "gay" wouldn't have meant anything to them.

GOLDSTEIN: That means they moved in the straight world.

BALDWIN: They moved in the world.

While Baldwin accepts that the "gay world" has come about as a response to repression, and welcomes its potential to make life easier for gay men and women, ultimately he questions its usefulness, believing it imposes an unnecessary limitation. "It seems to me simply a man is a man, a woman is a woman, and who they go to bed with is nobody's business but theirs. I suppose what I am really saying is that one's sexual preference is a private matter."

Baldwin's point is one of liberation and justice. Comparing the fight with that for racial equality, he argues that it is a mistake to answer in the language of the oppressor. "As long as I react as a 'nigger', as long as I protest my case on evidence or assumptions held by others, I'm simply reinforcing those assumptions." Ultimately, he hopes that "gay" will cease to be needed or used, as "it answers a false argument, a false accusation". This is society's accusation of our pathology, that somehow our sexuality makes us a different kind of human. It is a presumption of categories based on sexual preference and a *right-to-know* into which of these categories you or I fit. Such a presumption is manifestly discriminatory.

Like Baldwin, I'm denying the validity of the question. I'm saying I have nothing to prove. "The world also belongs to me."

In his interview with Parkinson, Thorpe says that if he'd not been asked from such a young age, and so obsessively, about his sexuality then he might have felt comfortable about it earlier. Acts of presumption do not merely deny an individual agency; they impose a knowledge upon them that is either false or inaccessible to them. Either way, it is a violent imposition, and a disabling one. It presumes a knowledge about others that cannot be had. For sexuality is made up of many things, including fantasies and repressions. Such things are not accessible by others.

We cannot know the totality of someone's sexuality, in part because it is not the kind of thing that can be known.

In a discussion of *Othello*, Adam Phillips[17] describes Brabantio's inability to comprehend Desdemona's choice of a husband as a failure "to get it". He outlines our developmentally necessary illusion that we can know ourselves and others – an illusion that results in "transference" of this illusory knowledge onto others as a means of opening up the possibility and freedom of not knowing them. "Psychoanalysis as a treatment, is an opportunity to recover the freedom not to know or be known", and with that freedom comes the possibility of finding out what we may do together instead. He cites Stanley Cavell on *Othello* and the transformation of knowledge into acknowledgement. In much the same way, we cannot "know" the sexuality of others or ourselves "partly because they do not know about it themselves; and partly because it is not the kind of thing that can be known." If one of the functions of analysis is the reseparation of sex from knowing, then sexuality is not something to be known but merely acknowledged; rather than a knowledge of it, perhaps the best we can hope for is to reach an understanding continually made anew through experience. Phillips is of Baldwin's party when he suggests there is something intrinsically disordered about our cultural compulsion "to know" the sexuality of others:

> Only a world that prioritized knowing would need to give such excessive attention to the one thing that cannot be known about a person. Who their children fall in love with shouldn't make too much sense to their parents.

Thorpe was taken to task for saying in his autobiography that he was often "accused of being gay". I don't agree with those who took this as his implying homosexuality is a negative, an accusation. The repeated questions concerning his sexuality, the accounts that were at odds with his own *were* a form of accusation. For others to claim Thorpe was gay also implied he was dishonest; or, that he lacked an understanding of himself that was evident to others. Yet, this presumes not only that sexuality is a fixed truth, to be known and understood, but also that sexuality is something that can be known. Further, not only that we can *know* such a thing about ourselves, but that when we do know it we also *understand* it, can recognise it for what it means. Thorpe's statement years later that "the lie had grown too big" does not disavow his claim that he had been telling the truth originally. He can have been replying honestly then, only to be held captive by his earlier answers as he grew to understand what he knew. We do not treat other aspects of the human psyche as so readily accessible.

When I was fourteen, the BBC broadcast an adaptation of Anthony Trollope's *The Way We Live Now*. The romantic lead, Paul Montague, was played by Cillian Murphy. His wasn't an interesting character, on reflection, but when my sister asked me what I wanted for my birthday that year I was emphatic: I wanted the soft-leather, prospector's hat worn by Paul Montague. My sister got as far as speaking to the costume designer at the BBC and was informed it was an original and would cost £700 to remake. My sister asked me if I still wanted it. I have no idea what she would have done had I said yes, particularly given she was only twelve herself.

I now know it wasn't about the hat.

That being said, I don't think it was about sex either. I

wanted to be Cillian Murphy, to know Cillian Murphy, to have something of Cillian Murphy. Yet, I don't think I ever wanted to have sex with him. I simply can't *not* look at Cillian Murphy. He is my most enduring relationship.

My point is, I was not being dishonest at fourteen. Now I look back on that story as an awakening, a moment that revealed to me something of my desire. Quite *what* still remains a mystery, but it revealed that my desire was not conventionally heterosexual. And yet, I didn't understand this at the time – I knew *something*, but *what* I knew was lost to me. Which is why I think it entirely plausible that Ian Thorpe was not lying – that we can know things without understanding them, feel things deeply without knowing their meaning. That desire is written through us without its every word being legible.

We also construct narratives that give coherence to our lived experience. It is conceivable that after years of religiously watching any film starring Cillian Murphy, I've told myself the story of the hat to explain some incongruous experience. Maybe it was just the hat. We cannot be certain present explanations of our past feelings and desires were the reality at the time, so much as an explanation to meet our constant demand for a coherent self.

That first morning you woke to news that you now had a half-sister. She'd been born that night. And as you rolled in bed, cradling your bedhead, you cried, "But what if she has better cheekbones than I do?" I decided that this couldn't be in earnest, but actually I suspect it was. And I could have said, but no one has better cheekbones than you do. Or I could have said, but no one has better cheekbones than you do but Cillian Murphy – which you might have appreciated more.

Of course, the original, violent presumption is the heteronormative one that presumes everyone is straight until they declare otherwise. A further presumption is that the sex of an individual's current partner can tell us anything about their past or future partners. That this may be the case does not negate the damage done by a system that presumes to always *know*. What is required is a transformation of our illusory knowledge of others into an acknowledgement of their difference and our inability to know.

Maybe one day Tom Daley will say something that proves Dom Joly "right". But what is "right" here? If Daley were to say "There never will be a Mrs Daley" – and some may argue his engagement to Dustin Lance Black comes close – I remain unconvinced it would make Joly "right". Because he is still presuming foreknowledge and, with his use of "never", an absolute knowledge. Yet how can it be true if it was not true for Daley? Joly's column in *The Independent* can only seem to mean a presumption of knowledge either denied to Daley, or one he refuses to share. I can see no way in which that would be right: factually, morally or as an imperative to know.

All of this – the reporting of Tom Daley's YouTube

video; the Dom Joly article; the years in which the teen-age Ian Thorpe was interrogated about his sexuality as he stood poolside in just a pair of speedos; the sanctimonious pieces, years later, when Thorpe came out as gay – all of this says to me: this still matters. We, as a society, are not as okay with same-sex desire as we think we are. So no, I can only presume these journalists asked – and kept asking Thorpe – because they wanted to learn something about themselves. If this fifteen-year-old refused to play ball – was shy, reticent, private – then this was simply confirmation of their suspicions. Ultimately, the only conclusion I can draw about why it is so important to know the sexuality of another is to do with a need to differentiate and categorise based on a series of presumptions rooted in homophobia.

We need to know who they are.

Society demands a knowledge from individuals that demeans their human dignity, a knowledge that they may not have, a knowledge that we have no right to in the first place and a knowledge based in the "artificial divisions" of which Baldwin speaks. Gay people who demand such a knowledge of others out of a desire for solidarity are still reinforcing and accepting otherness.

If I seem to labour the point, it is deliberate. Do these approaches create an open, accepting environment for people to be themselves and expect to be understood? Or a limited, prescribed language, which places demands on people and does the opposite?

Foucault's theory of bio-power and the medicalisation of sexuality draws our attention to systems that prescribe, rather than describe, our experience. He argued that the act of confession does not reveal a self – a discovered nature – so much as a self constituted by the very categories used and required by the confession. In that sense, we are made by the categories, the language, at our disposal. But what if this language, these categories, fail to adequately describe our experience? With the increasing acceptance of gay relationships, it is those who fail to conform to either gay or straight who are left outside.

Late one night, in the midst of a discussion about this book, a professor asked me, "Well, if I take you inside now and gave you a hand job, that wouldn't make me gay would it?" Jane Ward asks a similar question in her book, *Not Gay: Sex Between Straight White Men*. Are those married fathers, who enjoyed mutual masturbation at boarding school, gay? Or merely bi? What of a woman who describes herself as bi because of a profound relationship when she was younger, but is now married to a man? What of the large number of ostensibly straight men who watch gay porn? Or lesbians who watch gay male porn?

Studies like Lisa Diamond's *Sexual Fluidity: Understanding Women's Love and Desire*[18] claim that fluid sexuality is more common amongst women than men. But Ward demonstrates that sex between men is every bit as prevalent as between women – yet straight, white men explain it away as bonding, ritualistic experience or sexual necessity. She finds married men having sex with each other in public toilets or parks; hazing rituals in fraternities and the military; sex between bikers; straight men using online personal ads to find other straight men as jack-off buddies; other men looking for sexual contact as a means of reclaiming past forms of intimate, masculine bonding.

Asserting difference is a decision. And it is not a neutral decision either. The criteria we use to demarcate difference result in different answers. To categorise is a choice, as are the criteria we choose to categorise by. How do we define "homosexual" – by behaviour, self-identification or other criteria? And how, then, do we distinguish between homosexual and bisexual? A recent study[19] found that even (supposedly) scientific measures of bisexuality are deeply flawed. Western health surveys often measure sexual orientation. However, rather than taking self-identification or lifetime sexual behaviour as indicative of someone's sexual orientation, many surveys rely on short-term (often a year) behavioural classifications of sexuality. Those who only report same-sex partners in the last year are classified as homosexual, those who only report opposite-sex partners are classified as heterosexual, and those who report both same- and opposite-sex partners are classified as bisexual. However, this mandates that any self-identified bisexual must have slept with at least two people in the specified time period, otherwise they will be misidentified as gay or straight. Furthermore, if homosexual or heterosexual behaviour can be determined based on reporting of just a single sex partner, but bisexual behaviour can only be determined by reporting a minimum of two partners, "then by definition we are classifying 'behaviorally bisexual' to mean having more sexual partners than heterosexual or homosexual participants are defined to have." The shorter the time period, the greater the potential bias. Incredibly, the increased number of sex partners among bisexuals, mandated by this act of classification, has even been reported as a study finding! The myth of bisexual promiscuity may originate from nothing more than a classification bias!

We also see different answers depending on whether we frame the question of sexuality as binary categories or on a continuum. A 2015 survey on sexual identities by the UK Office of National Statistics[20] showed an increase of 45% over three years of young people, aged sixteen to twenty-four, who identified as bisexual. A higher number, 1.8%, identify as bisexual than those who identify as gay or lesbian combined. Yet, the total number of queer young people is still a small proportion of the overall population, making up only 3.3% of the survey. However, when YouGov[21] asked people to place themselves on the Kinsey scale for sexuality, 19% of all adults identified as something other than wholly heterosexual or homosexual. This figure rose to 43% of those aged between eighteen and twenty-four. When including those young adults who placed themselves as exclusively homosexual on the scale, half of eighteen to twenty-four year-olds stated they were in some way queer. The emphasis or distinctions by which we categorise difference result in different answers.

Kinsey's own reports found that 46% of males and 28% of females engaged in both homosexual and heterosexual sex, or "reacted" to people of both sexes throughout the course of their adult lives. Kinsey's results were found through a series of questions, while the YouGov poll merely asked people to plot themselves on the scale. This may explain why, with the exception of the younger generation, the poll results were slightly lower than those found by Kinsey. Even so, I'm surprised so many UK adults were as honest about sexual behaviours that confounded the usual binary identities.

The Kinsey scale also draws our attention away from simply the sex act to a range of sexual behaviours, desires and fantasies. This more accurately reflects sexuality as a range of experiences and feelings. Yet some have criticised the YouGov poll for not being explicit as to what constitutes same-sex experience. They argue that some respondents may only have kissed someone of the same sex. But this polices the boundaries of sexuality. It creates a hierarchy of sexual acts by which we judge the "seriousness" of an individual's transgression from their "usual" category. Such an argument is revealing in the primacy it places in binary categories over an individual's own sense of the importance of their desire and actions. It also begins an invidious process of interrogating their acts, feelings and fantasies. Again, this strikes me as an implicitly homophobic response – whether enacted by gay or straight people.

Whether this constitutes sex, kissing or merely sexual fantasy, what is significant is the number of people who *feel* their same-sex and opposite-sex attractions to be suitably significant as to report them. It is not up to us to tell them that somehow these feelings are insignificant.

David Halperin[22] observes that "the very notion of homosexuality implies that same-sex sexual feeling and expression, in all their many forms, constitute a single thing, called 'homosexuality'." The fact we have decided to categorise same-sex behaviour as something "other" is itself a choice. Not only do we make gender the defining characteristic – itself a contested area – but we presume to know what the gender of somebody's lover says about them both. Why have we chosen this characteristic when it may not reflect the greatest commonality of sexual desire? As Halperin asks, "Is a gay woman into S/M more like a gay woman who is not, or a straight woman who is?"

And maybe this is where we go wrong, or at least where we encounter problems: because homosexual, as a noun, can gather up many people who have at one time or another breached the rigid codes of heterosexuality. Yet, this blanket noun is problematic because many of these people are not exclusively homosexual. They are not exclusively heterosexual either. But our current language means any slight, any slippage from the (far too) high altar of heterosexuality, results in a simplistic other-ness.

The terms homosexual or bisexual would have meant nothing to the Ancient Greeks, the Renaissance Floren-

tines or Elizabethans, to Shakespeare or Homer. Homosexuality is not a category that easily crosses continents
nor centuries. In Renaissance Florence, two-thirds of
the men who had reached the age of forty had at some
point been implicated in a charge of sodomy.[23] The
problem was so pervasive that between 1432 and 1502
an "Office of the Night" was established to investigate
and prosecute cases. In a city with around forty thousand inhabitants, as many as seventeen thousand were
incriminated at least once for sodomy, with around
three thousand convicted. The practice was so wide-
spread amongst all social strata that the "Office" was
eventually disbanded.

Same-sex desire was not recognised as something different by ancient and early modern societies. They
understood a man's love of women and young men as
concomitant – not exclusive – desires. In this sense, they
are universal. Accounts, dating back to antiquity, detail
debates in which men argue over whether women or
boys are the superior sexual object choice. As Halperin
observes, these debates are prefaced on the sense of a
preference or taste, not a fixed sexual identity:

> They are presented as the outcome of conscious
> choice, a choice that expresses the male subject's
> values and preferred way of life, rather than as
> symptoms of an involuntary psychosexual condi-
> tion. The men who voice such preferences often
> see themselves as at least nominally capable of
> responding to the erotic appeal of both good-look-
> ing women and good-looking boys.

Marriage was the social constant in these societies. However, rather than a union of lovers, it was a union of political, familial or moneyed interests. Love and sexual pleasure were reserved for extramarital affairs, be they heterosexual, homosexual or both.

The categories of gay and straight are not only a recent construct, they are also arbitrary. Various reports over the last hundred years show that significant portions of the population recognise their desire towards both sexes, often as much as 40% of the population across studies; yet we still maintain the pretence that sexuality is a neat binary of straight or gay. When including those with exclusively homosexual attraction, the ratio of queer people rises to around half the population: half wholly heterosexual, half in some way queer and a minority of those queer people exclusively homosexual. Yet this is very different to the picture constructed by our language of sexual categories, in which bisexuals are presumed to be the minority amongst gay and lesbian people. In part, this reflects a reticence on behalf of some to recognise their same-sex desire for fear of their heterosexual desire being denied them.

This is not about paranoia or privilege, but expediency. I recognise a period of my history, my experience, in which I wanted to keep my sexuality imperceptible, or at least quiet. This wasn't only for the usual reasons but a protective gesture towards my heterosexual desire. For as long as bisexuality is denied, as long as it is presumed that any man attracted to another can only be gay, then some of us will feel forced to suppress "signs" or overt "displays" of our homosexuality, not because of internalised homophobia but because to do otherwise would undermine our heterosexuality in the eyes of everyone. It is not desirable, but it is a negotiated response to an exterior pressure.

The first time I spoke with you, working your shift in the café – when you smiled, looked back and smiled again, when you told me you remembered me from the other day, and I asked you about your tattoos, the breaking sky between your thumb and forefinger, and the balloon on your neck, like Pooh Bear's – I believed you were flirting with me. I hoped you were. And later, when we went for a drink, you told me you were bisexual – we had that in common. I was surprised, I hadn't expected that. Then I realised the problem with "bisexual" is that we can't do it all at once. When you were flirting with me you weren't flirting with anyone else. And later, when you flirted with that girl in the club, you weren't flirting with me. In that sense desire appears exclusive. But it was still my mistake – to assume your flirting with me and my flirting with you meant anything other than that. It was only ever about each of us in that moment.

Simplistic categorisation is not limited to popular culture – it is also evident in the academy. Those biographies and historical accounts of the lives of queer people that don't deny their same-sex desire as merely "friendship", almost uniformly label their subjects as gay or lesbian. However, these are recent terms, which are often meaningless when applied to the past. Other academics employ a subtle form of erasure, naming subjects as homosexual, thus dismissing as inauthentic any other relationships in their lives.

Part of the problem is that, unlike some other descriptors, "homosexual" or "heterosexual" are exclusive categories. For example, Joe Moran's moving history of shyness describes Siegfried Sassoon as "homosexual, and a Jew, of Persian ancestry, who converted to Catholicism in later life".[24] While the other descriptors can sit alongside each other, complicating and enriching our understanding of Sassoon, "homosexual" can disavow parts of his life. As well as several relationships with men, Sassoon was also married, fathered a son and was suspected by his wife of having an affair with Vivien Hancock, the headmistress of their son's school.

In his book *Gay Lives*,[25] academic Robert Aldrich leaves little room for ambiguity when describing Carson McCullers as "lesbian in her temperament and her desires". This despite the fact that she was married to the same man twice and had what Aldrich euphemistically calls "liaisons" with many men. His claim is also unprovable – we can never know the totality of someone's desires. Similarly, while evidence suggests Duncan Grant's sexual relationships were almost exclusively homosexual, he lived with Vanessa Bell for more than forty years and fathered a child with her. Elsewhere, accounts describe Thomas Mann as gay, although he was married to Katia Pringsheim and the couple had six children. These were people whose desires were various and complex, not a simple matter of either/or.

During the campaign for equal marriage, countless editorials and newspaper columns argued in favour, citing historical examples of miserable homosexuals, forced into loveless heterosexual marriages to satisfy social mores. Undeniably, this was the case in some instances. However, it is fallacious for us to presume that this was so in all cases where a married man or woman also had same-sex relationships and attractions. To do so makes uniform assumptions about sexuality ("either/or" once again), while assuming a hierarchy of value. It presumes to know *all* a subject's desires; it then presumes to know the significance and weight of each – some are obligatory, others are real; it also weighs the values of desires differently; finally, it asserts a truth value as to a subject's sexuality based on all these presumptions, dismissing marriages and children as mere trinkets of a presumed "false life". This isn't simply a mediating of desire, it is a policing of it and an enforced categorisation based on a desire to root out difference.

While we cannot ignore the role of repression and denial in queer lives, our simplistic understanding of sexuality as binary and a discovered truth (coupled with a constant suspicion of denial) blinds us to the possibility that queer figures from the past may have been struggling as much with the uncertainty and conflict of various desires as with the pressure of social convention. To state, as some histories do, that there is something categorical about the sexuality of figures such as Thomas Mann, Carson McCullers, Virginia Woolf and Christopher Marlowe (to name only writers) is an act of erasure.

To call out a subject as specifically one thing or another is to deny that they were something else. To identify Mann as gay is to deny his heterosexuality and, thereby, to deny the totality of his experience. We cannot speak with such certainty of Mann, nor others. As argued above, in many cases it is not possible to speak with such certainty of ourselves. We are not privy to all the underlying secrets of our desires, nor their origins and motivations. To make such general claims on behalf of others, including historical figures, is an act of supreme arrogance. It is akin to walking through a late relative's home and claiming only two of their most cherished possessions ever held any significance for them. Such a statement says more about the significance of these things to ourselves. It is also homophobic in that it fixates on any same-sex act to the exclusion of all else; anyone who has breached heterosexuality must be forever othered.

Yet, at the same time, we can and must proclaim the universalism of same-sex desire within human history. We should affirm the lives of those individuals whose historic same-sex attraction has been erased, but this should also be possible without erasing another aspect of their lived experience. Garth Greenwell observed the problem as "that distinction between activism and artistry; being torn between the political efficacy – necessity – of affirming these artists whose same-sex attraction has been so vociferously denied, so it cuts through the noise of that denial, but at the expense of nuance."[26]

I remain firm that the political necessity should not mean one form of historic erasure is overcorrected by another. This isn't the turf war Marjorie Garber[27] cautions against, over the categorisation of historical figures as gay or bisexual; something more significant is at stake. It is about a wider understanding of sexuality that recognises the multifaceted and complex nature of human desire. The alternative is "pinkwashing" (more accurately reflecting the word's etymology), in which an individual's complex sexuality is effaced in favour of a simplistic homosexuality. Recognising the instability of binary sexuality issues a radical challenge to heterosexuality itself.

The increasing commodification of sex makes a virtue of rigidity and fixity in our sexual choices. When Greenwell spoke at Foyles (London, 2016) about cruising gone digital, he urged caution over a swipe-left culture that reduced human dignity. Apps like Grindr and Tinder deny the ability for desire to surprise us, as we become hung up on our pre-existing preferences. This can be reductive both to our freedom and experience. As Paul Goodman acknowledged, "It is damaging for societies to check any spontaneous vitality."

I'm intrigued as to whether something about recent gay male experience fetishizes categories. Besides the increasingly refined categories of top, bottom and versatile growing to include versatile top, versatile bottom, there are also the various types of sexual object choice: twink, jock, daddy, otter, bear. The list is ever-growing, such as the recent conflation of twink and hunk into "twunk".

I can see why labels are useful. I can see that the list of terms above provide an easy shorthand, as well as cultural signifiers, amongst people denied the language to adequately express their desire in heterosexual discourse. And yet, I can't help feeling they are only ever reductive.

Gay dating apps are strewn with discrimination on grounds of race or effeminacy (discrimination sometimes called out by other users). But such language reduces people to mere attributes and categories. Once again, it is laden with presumption. The casual racism of "no rice, no spice, no chocolate" is also evidence of what Herbert Marcuse warned against last century – sex and individuals reduced to capitalist commodification. But these terms are not purely the product of the internet age. Halperin and others have described the history of terms like "rice queen", "size queen". Arguably this is evidence of further acts of identity construction – markers of commonality and difference. That these terms do not seem to have such a plethora of equivalence within heterosexuality or lesbian culture is, one could argue, because they function as a response to the very policing and exclusion conducted by heterosexuality. But it is also my anecdotal observation that those gay men most prone to insist on categories like twink top or twunk bottom are also most likely to deny bisexuality and demand the binary division of sexuality.

Commodification is the logical extension of codifying sexuality. For those whose desire is more varied and open to change, the imposition of the binary asks us to make a false and permanent choice, to "pick a side". While for those whose desire seems fully realised, even mundane, it creates reassurance in never looking outside of predetermined types. It is not that we should expect desire to constantly surprise us, but that we shouldn't be alarmed when it does. The commodification of our sexual preferences rejects the notion that desire is open to change. A desire so overused, so well-worn, fails to surprise and loses meaning. It becomes a sexual manifestation of cliché.

To name people based on their sexuality, their race, their sexual role, reduces us to a mere attribute. It caricatures us. It is an artificial division, one that limits us and deprives us of the fullness of our human dignity. To accept such a name involves the loss of something. It makes that our defining characteristic at the expense of all else that makes us human. As Baldwin observes, this loss is not only a public one – it is also interior and deeply personal. "I was afflicted by so many labels I had become invisible to myself… I had to go away someplace and get rid of all these labels and find out, not what I was, but who."[28] We lose something in the act of accepting a limited definition of ourselves. We lose our common humanity.

In particular, does the act of naming our sexuality – our desire – erase that very part of its being that makes it what it is? The social and political imperatives for queer people to talk about themselves in a manner that is expedient ignore the complexities, nuance and variety that make us human.

Accepting the need to speak of our experience in such a reduced way to fight for equality is the first concession. And to me it already feels a concession too far.

The flipside of presumption is verification. If we are not presuming something about somebody, then we are verifying their authenticity. Anakana Schofield attacks the current literary trend for confessional fiction. Her argument is that readers and critics give greater respect to writers who can authenticate the experience they write about, but in doing so they devalue the imagination. When she was interviewed about her acclaimed novel, *Martin John,* Schofield found she was asked repeatedly whether the protagonist, a dangerous sex offender, was someone known to her; whether she was one of the brutalised, violated victims.

If I am a dangerous sex offender is my novel about a sex offender more valuable? Would the implied authenticity or authority actually raise its literary merit? I believe we are currently in an intellectual weather system where it would... not only does the biographic usurp the imagination, but the market demands the writer... provide it. Fiction has more market value if it's backed up by an additional justification for its existence.[29]

Not only does this speak of our *need-to-know*, our modern fixation with certainty, but once again it is an act that attempts to package up and separate out human experience.

When I heard Schofield speak at the London Review Bookshop (2016), she highlighted the dehumanising nature of verification. Our need, when talking about child refugees in Calais, for example, to verify the truth of their experience is a subtle way of distancing ourselves from their humanity. "Are they a *real* refugee?" "Are they *really* Syrian?" In some sense, what we want to know is how we can be let off the hook. By placing a burden of responsibility on others to verify the truth of what they say about themselves, we can reduce, or step back from, our own responsibility towards them as fellow humans. At the same time as demanding verification, we also objectify them, seeing them as somehow strange and different from ourselves.

In some respects, this also harks back to Baldwin's observation on the universalism of homosexuality. The question repeatedly asked about Schofield's novel not only devalues the role of the imagination, but also attempts to objectify her protagonist as something other, who could only have been depicted by someone with first-hand experience. The question is predicated on the very opposite of Baldwin's point: we want to know that Schofield *has* been the victim of a sex offender because we don't want to believe that she can be capable of such a leap of empathy and imagination. Far from wishing to believe that we are each of us capa-

ble of anything, good and ill, we want to divide humanity up into acts from which we can feel safely set apart.
Witness the rigidity with which people, both gay and
straight, reject any notion that they could be otherwise,
in spite of the fact that the permanence of our sexuality and our feelings is not something we can be certain
about. We feel compelled to define ourselves in *opposition to* others.

People can be obsessive about verifying and authen-
ticating the sexuality claims of others. On one occa-
sion, a nurse asked for my sexual orientation and I told
her I was bisexual. "But would you consider yourself
more straight or gay?" she asked. I replied that I didn't
see it like that – in fact that was rather the point. But
she was adamant. "But what proportion?" she asked.
"What percentage of partners either way?" I have been
met with variations of this question several times, but
actually they are all the same question: *Are you really
gay?* The question seeks to verify the "truth" of my own
account and determine my true, innate sexuality.

Participants in one study[30] questioned the legitimacy
of bisexuality on the basis that most people would
have a preference or a greater prevalence of same- or
opposite-sex attraction. We are so invested in the idea
of binary sexuality we dismiss an individual's attraction to both sexes in preference for a "good enough"
identity based on the proportion of their partners either
way and a perceived preference for men or women.
Some people are prepared to dismiss sexual behaviour,
sexual attraction, sexual identity, all for the sake of the

increasingly shaky categorisation of gay or straight.

Those men and women who fail to conform to binary sexuality are not only accused of bad faith; we are asked to verify our experience, often merely to confirm the presumptions made by our interrogator. I've been asked by relative strangers when I last had sex with a woman; how often; whether this was penetrative sex rather than "merely intimacy". Apparently dating doesn't count. To me this demonstrates how low the bar is set for a man to be excluded from heterosexuality: a single kiss with a man can be taken as symptomatic of closeted homosexuality, yet the verification of bisexuality demands a detailed sexual history, which is often still insufficient.

On the other hand, women are presumed to claim bisexuality merely as a means of attracting male attention. Patriarchal presumptions are such that a man who has willingly chosen even once to deviate from the masculine norm is forever suspicious and othered; while, conversely, any woman who rejects the norm is forever suspected of not being wholly serious. As Ruby Tandoh brilliantly put it: all roads lead to men.[31] This suggests to me a subtle form of homophobia coupled with a deeply anxious need to reinforce binary sexuality. It presupposes a truth – a fixed, known truth – that the object is aware of, concealing, and that the interrogator must reveal.

Dennis Altman argued that we need to accept the part of ourselves that is sexual, and that this includes all varieties and potentials for ourselves. Such a thing means accepting our homosexual potential – and heterosexual potential – which in a way, seems to me an acceptance that this is not something that can be truly known.

An acceptance of our sexual potential to simply love, without mandating a category, is about an openness to the individual – that we love them for *who* not *what* they are. Altman predicted that such a stance would be:

> deplored by the custodians of the old values. In their book *Growing Up Straight* the Wydens make exactly this point (though not, of course, as advocates): 'The more acceptable the viewpoints of organized homosexuals become the more likely that we will see the growth of an ever less covert and more accepted Gay World.'[32]

As my experience in the café demonstrated, an understanding of desire that does not make presumptions but merely accepts the experience of desiring an individual *in that moment* results in greater freedom than categorisation. It is not about everyone being secretly bisexual, but allowing sufficient freedom that anyone might be.

In *Giovanni's Room*, when Giovanni cries, "Oh, the faces in that bar, you should have seen them, they were so wise and tragic and they knew that *now* they knew everything, that they had always known it, and they were so glad that they had never had anything to do with me,"[33] it is not real knowledge, nor real wisdom, they possess, but prejudice. The knowledge they presume of Giovanni is wrong. But the book makes repeated appeals to knowledge: on the one hand there is self-knowledge, which the narrator refuses; but on the other there is a public knowledge that is presumed and always wrong. And that is the kind of knowledge that cannot be had, that Baldwin shows does not exist, or at least means nothing. Giovanni tells David, "You are the one who keeps talking about *what* I want. But I have only been talking about *who* I want."

Our obsession with "the homosexual", the noun Baldwin denies, results in the narrator turning his back on love. But love of a man or woman is not clean, nor does our cultural fixation *mean* anything. The narrator says they are both men; what can happen between them, he asks. Giovanni tells him he knows what can happen, that is why he is walking away. What can happen is love. David is fixated by the category; he cannot forget that Giovanni is a man; Giovanni tells him that it is not the what, but the who that matters. This echoes Baldwin's observation about a self-knowledge of who, rather than what, we are. It is predicated on an acceptance of our common humanity and a particularity that is as unique as our individual experience.

As gay liberation has challenged the prescription of heteronormativity, increasing numbers of people – especially the young – are comfortable in accepting the multiplicity of their sexual lives, homosexual and heterosexual. It is the elevation of *who* over *what*. Gay liberation liberates heterosexuals too. Yet the custodians of the old values are not only heterosexual. Some gay men and women question the sincerity of those who claim a greater degree of sexual fluidity. There is a suspicion that being bisexual is merely "cool". Yet, the YouGov poll shows that across all adults, even those who plotted themselves as a one on the Kinsey scale ("predominantly heterosexual, only incidentally homosexual"), 23% had had a sexual encounter with a member of the same sex, while the figure rose to 52% of those at level two ("predominantly heterosexual, but more than incidentally homosexual"). Far from a mere fashion statement, the results demonstrate a genuine continuum of sexual desire and behaviours.

While I can understand the difficulty for those who had to fight past battles in accepting a greater degree of freedom and movement in how people define their sexuality now, that does not legitimate a new imposition of value or presumption about others as a result. Those of us standing on the shoulders of queer people who fought past battles are like children rejecting our parents. Children do not always recognise nor thank their parents for what they have done, nor for the sacrifices they have made. But neither should a child grow up being expected to meet their parents' idea of them. A parent cannot constantly remind the child of what they have sacrificed, with an invoice demanding the child must live like them.

Such a refusal to allow others to define themselves, to ascribe them the same degree of human dignity we expect for ourselves, is what Baldwin and many others fought against. Greater expression and freedom to love who and how we choose is the victory that gay liberation strove for. It should be celebrated, not denounced as dubious by the very people who fought to acknowledge all love's equal value.

Sexuality can be as vigorously policed by gay people as well as straight. Julie Bindel believes bisexuality is "increasingly used as a soft substitute for lesbian or gay".[34] Rather hyperbolically, she describes this as "almost an erosion of our identity". Such a statement defines bisexuality as both separate from and inferior to other expressions of queer desire. It further categorises desires and places them in a hierarchy of queer exceptionalism.

Citing several recent celebrities – including Daley, as well as Lady Gaga and Jessie J – Bindel claims that all of them "seem to be concerned with reassuring the general public that they are still attracted to the opposite, as well as the same, sex." This is a mirror of the suspicion and presumption demonstrated by Dom Joly. Rather than accepting that Daley and others are simply asserting their own *truth,* Bindel, like Joly, assumes their statements must be false and acts of bad faith. Bindel is also mandating an oppositional, radical, queer identity for all gay and lesbian people, regardless of how they feel. It suggests a superiority in difference – in which our shared humanity, with queer and non-queer alike, is less important than our difference. It transforms sexuality into a political statement of assimilation or difference, over a simple account of personal truth.

If one must trump the other, then I go for truth every time.

When Bindel says, "Jessie J is supposedly bisexual, but the rumours and suspicions point towards the idea she is simply a lesbian marketed in a way so as not to alienate straight men", I am disappointed that such a champion for women and gay people should be policing someone else's sexuality by elevating "rumours and suspicions" over an individual's own account of themselves. Undoubtedly, the forces of capitalism may mean a celebrity is cynically advised to conceal. However, I'm discomfited at the idea that suspicion should be treated as anything like fact, particularly publicly. Jessie J does not owe any of us an account of herself. Such a demand demeans our dignity, as Baldwin outlined. Once again, this is presumption as knowledge, coupled with a suspicion of all who deviate from the heterosexual norm. Are straight people so anxious about difference, gay people so desperate for affirmation, that we should suspect and interrogate the desires of others?

Bindel suggests bisexuality is somehow an insufficient form of queer. However, bisexuality does not somehow mitigate same-sex attraction in the eyes of homophobes; we are not less in solidarity, nor less in danger, because we also have opposite-sex attraction. If I hold my boyfriend's hand in the street, I'm just as vulnerable to the presumptions of gay-bashers as any other queer person.

There were times we were out and I'd be self-conscious, look-ing for where the first punch would come from, the first shout of abuse. I was on my guard and therefore restive and absent from you, as you rested your head on my shoulder as we took the last tube, on the weekend before Christmas. I wanted to enjoy it but I couldn't. I suppose I feared retaliation, accusa-tions of provocation. And all the time I wrestled with myself and my fear, I was pulling away from you.

It wasn't just me. On the way out that night, we passed four, drunk guys in tracksuits and you confided loudly that you were used to gauging the strength of white men in sportswear relative to your own. That none of them had thighs to take on yours. I knew that to be true. But I felt sad you should have to assess it. That we both did. And that you had enough experience to know – from the kicks and punches you'd endured before. You reckoned you had the beating of them.

I knew I didn't but that if it came to anything this was my turn. I felt that if anyone was getting a kicking it deserved to be me. I don't know why I assumed you'd have run, but I'd have wanted you to. No, this one is mine, I thought. My turn – for all those years of being less brave, and more fortunate, than you. Being oh-so-very-quiet. Hoping that no one would notice. That was why I deserved a kicking.

Although you confided, really you were shouting. It was a kind of boast. "I can assess the muscle strength of white men in sportswear." We were at the end of the carriage, hold-ing onto the handles with a breeze anything-other-than-fresh blowing in from the central window at the end of the com-partment. That breeze was relief that they hadn't followed us onto the train. And, of course, that night we were fine. But I feared for the one time we might not be, and every time I did *so, somehow I pulled away.*

In 2012, the actress Cynthia Nixon was widely condemned by gay-rights groups for claiming she "chose" to be in a lesbian relationship. Activists argued that this would stoke the religious fundamentalists seeking to undermine gay rights. Such an argument rejects Nixon's own understanding of herself in favour of political expediency.

Ward reckons that the activists who condemned Nixon did so, not for her statement about herself, but for telling the American people that sexuality is fluid and open to change.

> The controversy over Nixon's comments make clear that the lesbian and gay movement has largely succeeded in linking gay pride and gay rights with adherence to sociobiological narratives, and conversely, and perhaps unintentionally, it has also succeeded in equating more fluid and/or queer accounts of sexual desire with homophobia and collusion with the religious right.

To accept the activists' argument makes a concession. It concedes the validity of the question and claims no queer person would choose to be as they are, so they should therefore be granted equal rights. It also fails to accept an individual's account of themselves and mandates a language for sexuality, regardless of whether it accurately reflects their experience. This language mandates it as politically incorrect to say queer people may change – not by an act of will, but because sexuality can be transient. Then, rather than it being offensive to make the presumption that anyone whose sexuality later changes was previously living in denial, it becomes offensive *not* to make such a claim.

Such an approach falls into the trap described by Baldwin: rather than seeing all desire as equal, our defence of same-sex desire accepts the terms of the oppressor. And in so doing, we erase and limit the lived experience of the many, past and present, whose sexuality and understanding of themselves is more complex and nuanced than our current terms allow. Essentially, this is heteronormativity enlisting gay people in the policing of heterosexuality.

The closest we ever got to a row was over Ben Whishaw. We were in a pub, overlooking a street wet with rain, and you said you were irritated that Ben Whishaw had not been honest about his sexuality. I felt he had, that his refusal to answer one way or another – his statement that it is about a person – was his answer. But this wasn't clear enough for you. I think you felt he was being vague to the point of deception; and yet, when he married a man, he was being fêted as some sort of pioneer. I disagreed with so much of this: being asked explicitly if you're gay and refusing to answer but stating it is about a person seems to me a categorical rejection of heteronormativity. Saying it is about a person, in response, seems to me pretty queer; it strikes me as an acknowledgement, without accepting further invasion into his privacy or simple categorisation. Above all else, it struck me as honest. I said words to this effect. I remember you being exasperated, but I don't remember how the argument ended. I think we just moved on. I sensed we both had competing requirements – you for an unabashed recognition and solidarity, and me for a recognition of nuance and the rejection of an imperative to let everyone in. It is vital to me to resist opening the door to my soul to allow others to walk in. But while I have my own reasons for that feeling vital, I appreciate your own experience may have had different priorities. We let whatever difference sit between us. Then you smiled, picked a giant Yorkshire pudding up off your plate, and held it up to the sun to better take a photograph on your phone.

Yet, the activists who attacked Nixon mandate their argument as a moral imperative. They claim that to argue that sexuality might be socially constructed or given to change is to aid the very forces that oppress and discriminate against gay people. However, as Ward observes, the science around innate sexuality is also reliant on subjective categories and various dubious presumptions:

To insist that one is born heterosexual or homosexual is to engage in science that hinges on a very historically recent and specifically European-American understanding of what being gay means. Is anyone who has ever experienced same-sex desire gay? What do we mean by desire? If one needs to act on such desires, how many times does one need to do so? How much do the circumstances or cultural contexts matter? Is the story different for women and men?

...As Rebecca Jordan-Young illustrates, these are

precisely the basic questions that have plagued the burgeoning field of "sexed brain" research, resulting in three primary measurement errors: overly simplistic and contradictory definitions of sexual orientation, which are often rooted in early studies of animal behaviour and extrapolated to human sexuality; inconsistencies in the way homosexuality and heterosexuality are measured in men versus women; and lack of consensus about how frequently, or to what degree, one must be "homosexual" (in acts, thoughts, and desires) in order to qualify as homosexual for scientific purposes.

As Baldwin predicted, by accepting the premise that sexuality is biologically determined, we risk capitulating to a homophobic argument that suggests such a desire is only acceptable if it is innate.

Increasing numbers of people believe sexuality is innate. 13% of the US population believed so in 1977, 31% in 1998, 52% in 2010. Gay rights activism accepted this line as a response to the homophobic right's attack on homosexuals and the prevalence of cure therapies. It seemed expedient to claim that sexuality was as immutable as race. What Appiah calls the racial fixation is now a sexuality fixation: the idea of a racial essence is now transferred onto the notion of an essence of sexuality. However, sexuality can be mutable but still resistant to change. Psychoanalysis and psychology tell us how untouchable aspects of ourselves can be from agency and willed direction. Sexuality can be resistant to "cure", while at the same time being transient.

A friend confided that one of the reasons he was sceptical about bisexuality was the encounters he had at school. Theoretically, he didn't have much issue with what I say. However, practically he did because of the numbers of people he claims are in denial. Growing up as a gay teenager, he struggled with the instances where a guy would flirt with him or kiss him at the school disco, only to see them with a girlfriend a few weeks later.

I'm sure all of us, straight or queer, recognise something of this story. Its universalism is what strikes me. There is a universalism to being disappointed in love, to feeling that a promise has been left unfulfilled.

Goodman touches upon this when he describes his feelings on being rejected.

> I don't complain that my passes are not accepted; nobody has a claim to be loved (except small children). But I am degraded for making the passes at all, for being myself. Nobody likes to be rejected, but there is a way of rejecting someone that accords him his right to exist and is the next best thing to accepting him. I have rarely enjoyed this treatment.

Goodman was bisexual and is speaking here of the particularity to the experience of being queer and being shunned by those you desire. However, his words also speak to something universal: a denial of dignity.

I don't believe that every one of those guys from the school disco is secretly gay, living in a loveless marriage. I suspect that many of them simply didn't like my friend enough – enough to pursue it, or enough to wrestle with the awkward questions about what it meant. And *those* are two different things. Because, many of us will have disappointed someone who liked us by not living up to the suggested promise of what might be. The difference, and it's not an insignificant one, is when someone feels unable to pursue what might have been because of the still-pervasive issues around sexuality.

This is a distinction it is often impossible for us to know, and therefore dangerous for us to police. However, a world in which individuals are free to act on each moment of desiring, without it being immediately assessed as a symptom of pathological difference, would treat such an individual with greater dignity. In doing so, we may afford them the chance to treat others with greater dignity too. In both instances, it is about *who* rather than *what*.

Greenwell beautifully evokes the particularity of queer exclusion in *What Belongs to You*, when the teenage narrator is rejected by his best friend, K., who turns away from him as "I felt him identify me as foulness".[35] The two of them have shared a moment of physical intimacy, which K. tacitly rejects when he gets a girlfriend and "catalogue[s] his feelings" to the narrator. This told intimacy has a dual function – it at once invites the narrator in, only to demonstrate that he is being shut out. Eventually, K. invites his girlfriend and the narrator over to his house, where the couple's "feelings were bright and open, sure of their place". This is contrasted with the experience of same-sex desire. When the narrator is asked to keep watch at the bedroom door, he finally has the realisation that he is there "not as guard but as audience". This is a common trope throughout literature: the queer subject as outsider – observer and recorder – of heterosexual lives.

But I *still* don't think this means that every teenager, nor adult for that matter, who has a same-sex encounter and leaves the other disappointed is nursing some deep, yet repressed, longing. That smacks of exceptionalism – our exception in being liberated, and cold comfort that rather than *us* being rejected we are being rejected by the perverse workings of a homophobic world. While such a thing can be undoubtedly true, to believe that it is always so denies others the agency to either be or understand themselves with the same kind of clarity we claim for ourselves. Such policing always presumes false consciousness in others, never our own. It is a perpetuation of a bad-faith approach to the world.

The painful thing to accept is that when I am rejected it is because I am not desired enough. That is *always* the case. Even in the instances where loving me means too big a risk, a confrontation with what desire for me may mean, it is still the case that desire for me is not enough to overcome that risk. The test is whether the rejection accords with my right to exist. A failure to treat me with that dignity is not limited to queer experience.

Of course, I was sad when I stopped hearing from you. Your silences weren't new, but the prolonged silence was. I hoped in vain there might be something I could say or do that would breach it. I knew this was all new to you. You were never less than honest. But I know that ultimately it didn't work out because I wasn't the person for you. To believe otherwise presumes a knowledge I cannot have and does both you and your current relationship a disservice. I believe you are happy and, as always, I marvel at the clarity with which you see life and, in seeing it, recognise what you need from it. It is that clarity that means I must accept that you knew you did not need me. That hurts. It hurts that my being in touch may cause you pain. I miss the promise you brought. I miss you.

If so many straight men are having sex with each other, then what does being straight even mean? Ward describes it as a tautological proposition in which heterosexuality is constructed, not through heterosexual sex, but "through articulation of investment in heteronormativity". To these men, homosexuality is something "other", which has nothing in common with their own same-sex behaviour, which they often take as an expression of their inherent masculinity.

Ward draws attention to the inconsistency that means while masculinity "is normally imbued with extraordinary agency", when it comes to homosexuality this is not the case. She argues that patriarchy and rape culture have relied upon a version of masculinity that sees men as more animalistic and with less sexual agency than women. Gay men, she claims, are most likely to see their sexuality as innate, while straight men are likely to excuse their homosexual contact as beyond their control, be it the result of situation (for example, a prison term), a deep need for masculine friendship or driven by ritual. Ultimately, beliefs in the difference between male and female sexuality reinforce the gender binary and the hetero-homo binary at the same time.

To those who argue we should take these excuses seriously, I say that to accept heterosexuality as contingent on its constant fulfilment and performance demonstrates its fallibility. Whatever the reasons, the clear definite lines – the border between heterosexual and homosexual – are shown to be porous.

In my previous work on sex in prisons, I was surprised that instances of homosexual behaviour by straight inmates were dismissed as merely "situational homosexuality" or "opportunistic homosexuality". These excuses were used by the participants themselves, prison staff, reform organisations and academics. Yet, the descriptions are often based on tired, old stereotypes: the men are getting sex in whatever way is available to them; the women are replicating cosy, domestic relationships. The presumption is never turned on its head: rather than men and women acting out same-sex desire out of necessity, some environments may normalise same-sex impulses that participants usually feel unable to act upon. The meaning of "opportunist" is denied its full force – rather than this same-sex behaviour being somehow unreal, it is a response to an opportunity, a situation in which participants feel they can *get away with it*.

I don't make a claim as to which of these arguments is true or more compelling. It may differ case by case. It may be a bit of both. But the presumption in favour of heterosexuality is, itself, revealing.

Many contemporary theories seem to ignore the most obvious explanation for same-sex contact: people have homosexual sex because they want to. Are the excuses, we may ask, to preserve the illusion that same-sex attraction is rare, unnatural, an aberration? That some behaviour may be explained away as necessity or even defended as an ironic display of heterosexuality, distinguishes it from "real" homosexuality, which is then made truly "other", deviant and uncommon. These narratives prop up binary sexuality, in service to a belief in the crumbling edifice of heterosexual primacy. As Ward states:

> Accounting for straight men's sex with men demands imaginative scenarios, elaborate frameworks, and lists of countless circumstances and situations that diminish male sexual agency... Aside from the evident problem of denying straight-identified men an agentic path to homosexual sex, these rhetorical manoeuvres betray the pitfalls of the heterosexual/homosexual binary more generally. For one, they illuminate the fragile and tautological construction of heterosexuality and homosexuality.

Writing in the seventies, Altman claimed "few homosexuals will deny their straight component", arguing that this demonstrated an understanding of the universalism and complexity of sexual desires. However, with the increased investment in innate sexuality, that is no longer the case. Some feel a challenge to innate sexuality an existential threat. Ward documents the vitriolic response she received from some gay men to a blog post she wrote concerning constructionist views of sexual desire. Some called her a "fucking whore", others a "stupid cunt"; some cited Diamond's work to suggest that female desire is relational and flexible, while male desire is fixed and biologically determined. This leads Ward to wonder why gay men should be so particularly invested in this narrative, contrary to the evidence. She concludes that the patriarchal structures that equate male homosexuality with femininity are so pernicious, gay men feel a greater legitimacy if their sexuality is seen as biologically determined, as opposed to an abdication of male privilege or a failure of masculinity.

Rather than, as she claims, an investment in heterosexuality, I believe the distinction is rooted in an investment in the problematic construction of masculinity.

Altman saw "a marked connexion in our society between the repression of bisexuality and the development of clearly demarcated sex roles". Drawing upon Marcuse's work, Altman argued that Western societies have repressed sexuality by denying our inherent bisexuality – Freud's polymorphous perversity – and removing the erotic from all areas of life other than the explicitly sexual. The denial of our bisexuality, he claimed, is rooted in a capitalist, dehumanising tendency to categorise, in particular "the very clear-cut concepts of masculine and feminine that dominate our consciousness and help maintain male supremacy". In such a scenario, homosexuality is an affront to the way society organises itself.

This is evident in the near-universal condemnation of men enjoying the passive role in homosexual sex. In Ancient Greece and Renaissance Florence, no man was meant to *enjoy* taking on the passive role: the younger man was only meant to do it for the status and prestige it would confer; while the older man was only meant to enjoy the active role. To enjoy the passive role was a sign of degeneracy. Passivity was equated with femininity.

Misogyny has shown itself more durable than homophobia. In many societies, it was not same-sex desire that was deemed inferior, but the feminine. In early modern England, it was an excessive love of women that was thought to cause effeminacy, not a love of young men. For example, in his epigram "The Juggler", John Donne's speaker is challenging convention by *not* acknowledging the superior masculinity of the boy-loving addressee:

> Thou call'st me effeminate, for I love women's joys;
> I call not thee manly, though thou follow boys.[36]

The enduring value is femininity as inferiority.

Halperin believes one of the benefits of the emergence of the homosexual as a distinct category is that it does away with a sexual hierarchy between the participants. He observes that the sex between men of Renaissance Florence is "sex as hierarchy, not mutuality, sex as something done to someone by someone else, not a common search for shared pleasure or a purely personal, private experience." The emergence of a homosexual identity marks a shift from classifying sexuality in terms of the penetrated and the penetrator, to one based on sexual object choice.

While this is clearly a positive shift, I believe Halperin romanticises the extent to which it is the case. As Ward catalogues, straight men see their sexuality in opposition to homosexuality precisely because of a perceived difference in their maintenance of masculinity. At the same time, parts of gay culture – "masc for masc", for example – make uniform assumptions about femininity and what it means to be exclusively passive. As mainstream homosexuality increasingly seeks to ape aspects of heterosexuality, the demarcations of heterosexuality are being visibly recreated by their gay counterparts.

I remember as a teenager being turned off by the straight pornography that always depicted the woman as a passive recipient of sex and, often, one violently used in the sexual fantasy of the man. This was not sex as a meeting of desire, mutual pleasure or shared intimacy, but an act done by one to another. Then, gay male porn seemed refreshing in its apparent equality. Young men would kiss, suck each other off and maybe fuck each other, but the physical language was not fixated on one as agent of their own desire and the other merely the passive receptacle for it. Now I see much gay porn replicating the excesses of its straight counterparts: an increase in the fetishizing of rape fantasies, the playing out of sex as done *to* someone else, or, at its most general, the bottom used and abused as a mere vessel for the dominant, active man. The language of such gay male culture seems to recreate the very misogyny I was looking to escape.

However, just as homosexuality may replicate the demarcated roles of heterosexual sex, the opposite can also be true. Queer sex has the potential to liberate heterosexuality from its prescriptive limitations. In *Bluets*, Nelson talks about a past boyfriend and how "It was around this time that I first had the thought: we fuck well because he is a passive top and I am an active bottom." This passing sentence felt like a liberation. The idea that queer sexuality can influence and even become straight sexuality, that the fluidity of roles and a rejection of the "norms" of gender in sex, that biology is not destiny should be true of the bedroom as much as anywhere else, thrills me. That the Edwardian understanding of sex I was brought up with should be smashed up by, of all things, homosexuality and resulting queerness, made me feel hopeful for my heterosexuality in a way I never thought possible.

You told me about a song you were writing. You wanted it to differ from the usual, for the man to be hesitant, uncertain about his attraction for the woman. Rather than cool and assured, he was to desperately hope she would take the lead. You never said, but I wondered if this man was you. I understood that and recognised it in myself. That there is a cultural presumption about men who aren't sexually assertive. I told you about a straight friend of mine. That because he's gentle and softly-spoken people have asked if he is gay. And what an indictment this seems against heterosexual men. Or society. That for a man to be kind and gentle to women means he can't desire them. And I could see that in you – a tenderness as you offered me a cigarette, a lightness to the tone of your voice, a hesitancy in your gestures. These things cause us trouble.

When pondering what instils fear and loathing in those who are anti-gay, Bindel reckons:

> The answer is, of course, that we present a clear threat, even if that is not our intention, to patriarchy and male supremacy over women and children. Patriarchy dictates the norms of sex, even.

This is why bisexual men have such a hard time and why Ward's research is so hard for many to comprehend. Social investment mandates an either/or for male sexuality, one that is deemed so necessary that society will label "repeat offenders" gay, regardless of their heterosexual acts, while the individuals themselves may dismiss any same-sex contact as irrelevant. The role of masculinity in demarcated sex roles can be seen in the historical superiority of the active male pederast over the passive sexual invert.

To claim that sexuality, particularly male sexuality, can be fluid – that a man may choose one moment to have sex with another man and the next to have sex with a woman, to argue that this is neither repression nor the result of accident or necessity – challenges the foundations of the patriarchy and the primacy it gives to a certain kind of masculinity.

Baldwin said homosexuals are targeted for abuse and violence precisely *because* others can see them as representing an aspect of themselves. This is also Altman's view. More challenging still, such a stance implies the rejection of difference, or at the very least a rejection of difference at the expense of solidarity. What matters to Baldwin is our common humanity, the universalism of desire. The act of focusing on one type of desire as pathological and different is oppressive.

Male bisexuality is a challenge to both heterosexuality and masculinity. The reasons gay and straight people police the binary so rigorously is to preserve the illusion of heterosexuality and its primacy and normalcy. Fluid sexuality issues a challenge that these things are not fixed, are not either/or. It raises the possibility that there is no division. If rather than being invented, or symptomatic of denial, sexual attraction is varied and multiple for many – if not all – of us, then the heteronormative, patriarchal presumptions about homosexuality being other are challenged. At one and the same time, I can conform to the masculine paradigm of heterosexuality, while also choosing homosexual sex; I can engage in sex with a woman but as the passive party.

Gender roles break down too.

Previously, the homosexual issued a challenge to het-erosexuality. Now, the liminal bisexual poses a threat to the very notion of the hetero- and homo- binary and masculine and feminine roles. In challenging the pre-sumptions around masculinity, male agency and male sexual dominance, fluid sexuality threatens the pre-sumptions of superiority upon which masculinity rests. If a straight woman can be the power bottom or active top, if a man can choose to be passive with another man or with a woman, and another time active – the tradi-tional presumptions of value begin to crumble. The foundations of masculinity are challenged, the edifice on which notions of masculinity, male privilege and difference are erected are under threat.

"A minority," says George in Christopher Isherwood's *A Single Man,* "is only thought of as a minority when it constitutes some kind of threat to the majority, real or imaginary. And no threat is ever quite imaginary."[37]

I fail at masculinity. I recognise that my bisexuality means I fail to meet a masculine paradigm. But I've come to realise failure is the whole point of masculin-ity. We all fail, we can only fail. That is the point. Mas-culinity's power comes from the oppression we all feel at failing at it every day, our failure to be the men it demands of us. What we must accept is that, for mascu-linity, to be a man means to fail at being a man. Maybe then we can accept that masculinity is a pernicious thing and that being a man has fuck all to do with it. I may fail at masculinity, but I don't fail at being a man.

There is a growing challenge within studies of literature against readings – acts of critique – that inherently
presume bad faith. When Rita Felski[38] describes the
workings of critique she could just as easily be describing the predominant language and approach to sexuality:

> *Critique is secondary.* A critique is always a critique
> *of* something… But while secondary, critique is
> far from subservient. It seeks to wrest from a text
> a different account than it gives of itself. In doing
> so, it assumes that it will meet with, and over-
> come, a resistance. If there were no resistance, if
> the truth were self-evident and available for all to
> see, the act of critique would be superfluous. Its
> goal is not the slavish reconstruction of an orig-
> inal or true meaning but a counter-reading that
> brings previously unfathomed insights to light.

Felski goes on to say that critique is drawn toward
self-reflexive thinking – the constant imperative for
individuals to reflect, check for denial, and confess
again. The advocates of critique are engaged in a
"shared investment in a particular ethos—a stance of
knowingness, guardedness, suspicion and vigilance."

This has much in common with J.M. Coetzee's notion
of "hyperconsciousness".[39] Coetzee diagnoses this as a
particularly modern condition. Such a state, exempli-

fied by the underground man in Dostoyevsky's novel *Notes from Underground*, is characterised by a constant self-analysis, which always defers the point of resolution, searching for further levels of self-deception. "The tendency of self-consciousness is to draw out confession endlessly."

Coetzee's essay is concerned with confession and man's need for absolution in a secular age.

> Because of the nature of consciousness, Dostoyevsky indicates, the self cannot tell the truth of itself to itself and come to rest without the possibility of self-deception...Self-consciousness will not give him the answer, for self-consciousness in *Notes from Underground* is a disease.

The self can never reach truth, the only thing the self can reveal is the self. Therefore, self-confession can never reach a satisfactory endpoint – after every confession the self will begin to search for further degrees of self-deception and, having found further possible levels of denial and bad faith, it can make a further, preliminary confession, before the whole process begins again.

Coetzee's "hyperconsciousness" is a form of madness. It is futile but seductive, for it bears all the hallmarks of reason, even if it is irrational in its pursuit because the truth it desires can never be revealed. Coetzee's hyperconsciousness is remarkably like Simon Critchley's description of the workings of depression in *Notes on*

Suicide.[40] Our thoughts about the world, the rumination that can lead to suicide, bear all the hallmarks of reason: we rationalise our feelings, our predicament, but the thoughts are disconnected from our experience.

Foucault observes something similar in *Discipline and Punish*, noting that objects of disciplinary control internalise these norms until they become monitors of their own behaviour, "controlled as self-scrutinising and self-forming *subjects* of our own knowledge".[41] The result is self-policing in pursuit of a resolution that is not to be had. It is not to be had because the language and categories of "disciplinary control" fail to account for the fullness of our desires.

Once as I waited at St James' Park station, I found that I'd checked out three different guys who walked past me on the platform. I clocked this as my constant act of self-policing. The scepticism that was others', and is now my own, mandates this as evidence of my own homosexuality. Yet, as the minutes passed I realised that amongst these three men I had also checked out two women. The accusations of denial against me, from gay and straight alike, make me self-conscious and watchful for any signs that they are right. But the imperative to observe deviance is not watchful of heterosexuality; the policing of the border country is only concerned with homosexuality.

There has been much speculation over John Cheever's sexuality. That his same-sex desire troubled him to such a degree is taken, by some, as evidence that his *true* nature was homosexual. What I struggle with, and this is in some senses the bisexual's predicament, is the inescapable context in which my sexuality is situated. I understand that the more socially and culturally problematic our homosexuality, the more it becomes the only thing we can see. The greater the demand to see it, to own it and to understand it, the greater its import in our eyes.

I don't doubt Paul Goodman's bisexuality, in spite of the fact that his final essays do not include a chapter – a focalising – of his heterosexuality. I accept that he thinks about, writes about, his queer experience because it is problematized in society in a way that his heterosexuality is not.

I have struggled with this for a long time. My same-sex desire can, at times, fill my vision. But it is not because it is all I am, nor all I desire, but because of the calls to explain and make sense of it. This is not a demand placed on normative experience, for the simple fact that normative experience is normal. So at least some of the awesomeness of this aspect, this confusion, of my sexuality comes from outside – the exterior imperative to explain myself, to make sense of myself.

Therefore, I think it entirely possible that Cheever was genuinely bisexual, but that his same-sex desire troubled him so much that he became fixated by it. Equally, he may have been fixated by it because there was nothing else to see. But I don't know, we can't know.

I am a regular swimmer. Despite swimming regularly, I know there's something wrong with my technique. My local lido offers group lessons for those looking to improve. The coach told me the other week that the reason I struggle with the crawl is because I have a natural breaststroke kick. Even as my mind tells my body I should be pointing my toes and painting the wall, I keep resorting to the breaststroke on my legs. She told me, I see a lot of kids with a natural breaststroke kick. Did you never learn the crawl? I told her I had, but that in my early teens I did two hours swimming after school every day. Two hours of breaststroke. That must be it, she said. You resorted to the breaststroke because you have a natural breaststroke kick. I reckoned that maybe I developed the kick because of the ten hours a week I did of breaststroke. Maybe that way it became my body's default.

Which came first? Does it matter?

Just as with Cheever, I don't know which of these is true. Nor do I know how I can ever find out. But I do know that the importance of the topic comes from the remains of a social prejudice that demands an account of ourselves not required of others.

Those who fail to conform to gay or straight are left in the unfortunate position of being assessed and judged by society, while being told that they are least qualified to adjudge the truth of their feelings and desires because of the potential for repression and denial. Thus, the bisexual subject is at once asked to go back and confess again, while at the same time any answer that diverges from the exterior judgement is merely taken as further proof of the depth of self-deception.

When David Bowie was asked on the relatively liberal talk show, *Afternoon Plus*,[42] about his bisexuality in 1979, the host refused to accept his response. "You've been asked the question, whether you're bisexual or not," said Mavis Nicholson, "and you've never quite answered it." "Oh, I have," responded Bowie. "I said I was bisexual. That's enough."

> NICHOLSON: Does that mean, though, that you *really* are, or does that mean you are keeping something back—
>
> BOWIE: I've answered the question.

Yet, binary sexuality and our need for resolution means this is an insufficient answer, even now. To those sitting in judgement, the only issue is the extent to which an individual has had the strength and awareness to recognise and accept the "truth", seen as evident to the community. Those of us living within this state of radical confusion are constantly presumed to be acting in bad faith: by denying the binary we're in denial; if our sexuality later conforms to the binary then we must have been lying before. Our sexual desires are found to be genuine, or otherwise, but not on their own terms, but as assessed by an exterior gaze.

To always presume that the *only* issue those attracted to both men and women face is around their homosexuality denies the complexity of issues and problems people face in all aspects of their lives. Again, it is a subtle form of homophobia – always regarding same-sex desire as problematic and more so than any other issues an individual might face. The scepticism and suspicion around homosexuality elevates it to a role as the primary repression.

Altman describes a universal bisexuality, one he advocates on the grounds that same- and opposite-sex desire are *potential* components of us all, but also as a political act by which queer people win acceptance, as distinct from tolerance, "by a transformation of society, one that is based on a 'new human' who is able to accept the multifaceted and varied nature of his or her sexual identity."

> Homosexuals who like to point out that everyone is queer – "either latent or blatant", as one girl put it – rarely concede that everyone is equally straight, and that to repress the one is as damaging as to repress the other. It may be the historic function of the homosexual to overcome this particular form of repression, and bring to its logical conclusion the Freudian belief in our inherent bisexuality.

Yet, as Altman tacitly implies, suspicion around sexuality only ever works one way. Society is sceptical of those who claim to be attracted to both sexes for a whole variety of reasons, but chiefly because of our fixation with the possibilities of repression. We suspect that they are unreconciled to their same-sex attraction. Besides the usual anxieties around "coming out" and non-heteronormative sexuality, the narrative that regards desire as fixed and knowable demands constant confession and reassessment from those for whom sexuality is transient or simply not either/or. Sceptics of bisexuality subject others to a constant act of both interior and exterior hyperconsciousness, interrogating the sincerity of their "confession". It turns individuals into objects of critique. At the same time, by forcing bisexuals to interiorise the narrative of binary sexuality, it demands that we verify the truth of our claims, and treats us as something other than human.

The simplistic, cod-psychology of the press and public, which views repression and difficulty as the purview only of the homosexual, ignores the other myriad ways in which upbringing, trauma and crises can also result in problems with expression of opposite-sex desire. Altman speculates on the prevalence of heterosexual shame and stigma, albeit of a different order. This rings true to me, but society only polices it in instances of same-sex attraction. Arguably, in doing so, such a narrative may attempt to display an appreciation of its own oppressive strains. However, the manner in which it does so is prescriptive and continues to problematize same-sex attraction as intrinsically disordered, even if that disorder is only ever repression as a result of an externally enforced shame. We need to recognise that increasingly there are those with loving and accepting families for whom same-sex attraction is not the taboo it once was; while, at the same time, there are those who, for whatever reason, find their heterosexual desire difficult to explore, or difficult to reconcile with their same-sex attraction in a society that mandates either/or.

I know that heterosexual relationships have for me a different kind of baggage to homosexual relationships. I don't believe this makes one or the other "true". I know what I feel for those I've loved. But I also know what makes some things difficult. It's not always as simple as saying you have trouble reconciling yourself to same-sex attraction. Plenty of us have reasons to find our opposite-sex attraction difficult as well. There are plenty of ways it can be hard to be truly ourselves.

It was late, I was in Cork for a festival and I was drunk. I'd finished Just Kids *and texted you to say we'd lived and loved like Patti and Robert. I asked who is to determine significance; that we'd lived together while you were seeing your fiancé, but that that shouldn't erase the significance of our relationship, one that had been a marriage of its own. I guess, crassly, I was telling you I loved you. Which of course you knew. That all those nights we'd eaten in restaurants long after closing time, with waiters reassuring us they were happy for us to stay while they cleared the other tables around us; the years we'd lived together, every late afternoon drinking tea in the bookshop – that some relationships endure and have a profundity without or after sex. That sex itself is not an indicator of depth of feeling. Desire is not always requited nor acted upon. What I failed to say was simply: I love you. And that the book reminded me, with Robert painting the kitchen and Patti getting chocolate with the last of her wages, of me changing the door handles while you bought an Easter egg in the middle of January to keep out the dark and cold.*

The imperative for people to meet the binary – one that we internalise, as Foucault observed – can have a detrimental effect on the health of the men and women who fail to meet it. The need to know – the presumption of superior knowledge of the desires of others – results in greater mental health problems for bisexuals than their gay counterparts. A 2012 study[43] by Stonewall found that while 18% of lesbian women had self-harmed in the last year, the figure rose to 29% of bisexual women; 3% of gay men had attempted to take their own lives, while the figure amongst bisexual men almost doubled. The damage of an insistence on binary sexuality is real, but often these significant facts are overlooked.

Humans are not good with uncertainty. There was a time when I was so exhausted by uncertainty I considered coming out as gay, simply for the relief of certitude. That it would have been untrue seemed a small price to pay to have the matter resolved.

Similarly, I remember when you left my house in the early hours of a Tuesday morning. We'd drunk a bottle of wine and you'd put your head in your hands and said "I just wish I knew." I said, "Welcome to a whole world of hurt." Which was glib and unhelpful. It also wasn't true. I walked you outside. Then I ran back in to fetch the engine piston that I used as a paperweight and brought it out to you so you could feel the grooves where the piston had run amok and smashed into the inlet valves, leaving these raised, carved crescents of steel. You ran your fingers around them as though making out the words.

Your bike was off the ground, chained to wrought-iron railings above a wall – as though you had simply thrown it there and it had stuck. I believed you had it in you for that to have actually happened. And when you said goodnight, we both turned and watched a man walk down the street at this early hour and then, as though we'd both decided to take the risk, we kissed each other goodnight.

"That's the first time I've kissed someone with stubble," you said. "It's kinda cool." And you gave that smile of yours which could have melted the piston or thrown your bike.

Our act of checking, the fact of needing to look, that fear: that is political. But the kiss was not. It was simply a kiss.

Uncertainty can be unbearable – at once everything is open, and everything is denied.

When walking home from the Christmas pantomime in December 1817, John Keats got into a lengthy discussion with his friends, Charles Wentworth Dilke and Charles Brown. He later set it down in a letter to his brothers, George and Tom:

> ...several things dovetailed in my mind, & at once it struck me, what quality went to form a Man of Achievement especially in Literature & which Shakespeare possessed so enormously—I mean *Negative Capability*, that is when a man is capable of being in uncertainties, Mysteries, doubts, without any irritable reaching after fact & reason—Coleridge, for instance, would let go by a fine isolated verisimilitude caught from the Penetralium of mystery, from being incapable of remaining content with half knowledge.[44]

I confess, I have no conviction on this topic now. Except the conviction that self-doubt is something I have to live with.

What I have slowly come to realise is that, for me, sexuality is a permanent state of not knowing. The hyperconscious interrogation is futile – it will never reveal a satisfactory answer. I can never be certain that there aren't further levels of deception, just as I cannot be certain that, at the moment I think I have reached an understanding about myself, it will not be disrupted by some new person or event. Whether these anxieties are my own or the result of internalising social anxieties, these questions have become a part of my desire. Now I accept that this is my only answer, the only revelation: it is that I have no answer, there is only what I feel in this moment in time.

When you came with me to visit my father, you told me afterwards that every time I left the room he would begin to unburden himself of yet another family secret. No matter how many times you asked him to stop, he would keep on. You told him you weren't the right person for him to share all this with, but he was insistent that you know. We laughed at him later. When you told him you were moving out of our place, moving to Oxford to live with your boyfriend, he was pulled up short. "Boyfriend?" he asked. "But what will Michael do?" This only seemed to confirm he'd got the wrong end of the stick. And yet, looking back, I can't help feeling he maybe understood better than either of us.

I set great store by truth. I fear too much. I am fixated on it, searching for it. I never want to let it out of my sight. I am not such a stickler for it as Coetzee, I imagine, but I suspect it is all I am really interested in. At the same time, this fixation increasingly leads me to accept the impossibility of what it is I seek. Not that I don't believe in truth, nor that it can never be known. But I recognise the myriad ways in which I will never know and cannot know. That, in this sense, truth is always provisional. But seeking it is still worthwhile, for I hope that each time I correct myself, I may get a little closer, or at least reveal something previously hidden.

To be myself, I need to know myself. Yet I can never fully know myself and to accept that fact is to understand myself as I am. It is Baldwin's understanding of "not what I was, but who", an understanding of human complexity beyond simplistic categorisation. Self-knowledge is not fixed and unchanging, because *we* are not fixed and unchanging. My answer today about who and what I desire may not be my answer tomorrow. It doesn't make me a liar, it makes me human. Yet grace in the face of our humanity is sorely lacking.

Grace towards others is particularly lacking in the sphere of sexuality: grace in terms of self-knowledge; grace in terms of acceptance and belief in an individual's account of themselves; grace as knowledge to be revealed, neither willed nor grasped. Queer people are expected to have a fixed and uncomplicated understanding of ourselves of a sort never demanded of straight people.

Coetzee observes that Dostoyevsky's critique of confession brings us to the cusp of truth-telling as close to grace:

> True confession does not come from the sterile, analogue of the self or from the dialogue of the self with its own self-doubt, but…from faith and grace.

If the truth about ourselves cannot be reached through the rationalism of hyperconsciousness then we must accept, as Phillips observed, that maybe it is not knowledge to be had. At the same time, like Keats' negative capability, such an acceptance may demonstrate faith in alternative means to understanding. That act of being in uncertainties may be akin to grace.

Phillips argues that we use knowing what we want as a comfort, to avoid exposing ourselves to change. At the same time, we also construct false certainties as a means of dealing with frustration. Frustration is "something we are tempted to get rid of, something we crave false solutions to…an unbearable form of self-doubt." Again, the answer lies in inhabiting our not-knowing. Not knowing what we want may be our only path to change.

So, just as my sexuality, my *queerness*, is in part a refusal to live in public, a refusal to answer a question, it is also an acceptance that it is a question without an answer. It is an acceptance of being in uncertainties. By giving an answer that I could be all and anything, I refuse to answer the question. So, at one and the same time, this is my answer but it is also a refusal to answer. It is a refusal to answer both because the question should not matter and because there is no adequate answer I can give. If my sexuality were to change, if it were to move on, I don't believe I would answer any differently. In part because it is a faith of mine that this is not a fact about myself I can ever adequately know, but, as important, nor is it a fact anyone else has any right to. I won't answer because I deny the question itself. And *this* feels to me like a political and personal imperative.

There is an aspect of the bisexual experience that is problematic and means life can only be lived, rather than thought in the abstract. When I told my mother that I might as easily come home with a boyfriend as a girlfriend, she eventually snapped and said she didn't see why we needed to talk about it now – in the abstract. Why couldn't we cross that bridge when we came to it? I have come to see that, in part, she was right. Even as I know I can have an awareness of myself that doesn't have to be demonstrated in the here and now, I have also come to realise that the confusion, the flux, of my desires can leave me lost. They only become real when located in a person whom I desire *right now*. Then they cease to become a source of confusion but a place of knowledge and certainty.

This makes desire experiential. When discussing the systematic illusion of colour, Nelson writes, "We mainly suppose the experiential quality to be an intrinsic quality of the physical object",[45] and ponders whether it is also so with love. We believe our experience of the other to be a fixed, tangible thing. Yet, just as we experience the colour blue, our experience of desire is relativist; it is as informed by how we relate to blue, how we relate to it *in that moment*. Our response is as informed by us as it is by the object – "you don't read the text, the text reads you" – so this symbiotic relationship is an act of creation. It is meaning made anew in the act of experience. Or as Walt Whitman puts it in "Crossing Brooklyn Ferry":

> What is more subtle than this which ties me to the woman or man that looks in
> > my face?
> Which fuses me into you now, and puts my meaning into you?[46]

At times, I've wondered whether this book is an unwitting coming out. The writing I have always been most proud of, that has "worked", has been the writing that has been strange to me at the start and gradually made itself known. In that sense, I am revealing something to myself as I write. This is a further form of living in uncertainty: it is an acceptance of a creative impulse, the meaning of which is unknown, and may only reveal itself in the action.

In a discussion of Baldwin's essays and autobiography as a rehearsal for his fiction, José Esteban Muñoz[47] identifies Baldwin's final novel, *Just Above My Head*, as a work that exemplifies the theory of disidentification.

In Baldwin's novel, there are several characters representing the author in different ages, stages or aspects, as well as the novel's central themes of challenges to memory, narratives and genres. In writing so personally, autobiographically, Baldwin at once finds new identification with himself and his past, even as he makes it other. Muñoz writes:

> we begin to glimpse an understanding of fiction as "a technology of the self". This self is a disidentificatory self whose relation to the social is not overdetermined by universalizing rhetorics of selfhood. The "real self" who comes into being through fiction is not the self who produces fiction, but is instead produced by fiction. Binaries finally begin to falter and fiction becomes the real; which is to say that the truth effect of ideological grids is broken down through Baldwin's disidentification with the notion of fiction—and it does not stop here: fiction then becomes a contested field of self-production.

The creative act is also dislocated – disidentifed – as Baldwin's character Jimmy attests, "The song does not belong to the singer. The singer is found by the song." In this sense, our creation both belongs and does not belong to us. It is a form of revelation at once our own and with origins beyond our ken.

Inevitably, all experiences of desire are individual, except when they are abstract. Even if we recognise commonalities, whenever it is about a person it can only ever be individual. And yet, we insist on desire as being somehow categorical. Nelson observes:

> There are people out there who get annoyed at the story that Djuna Barnes, rather than identify as a lesbian, preferred to say that she "just loved Thelma". Gertrude Stein reputedly made similar claims, albeit not in those exact terms, about Alice. I get why it's politically maddening, but I've also thought it a little romantic—the romance of letting an individual experience of desire take over a categorical one.

I question why we should care if it is politically maddening. This is love as stance, not what it is: which is unique and personal. I can understand the political expedience of solidarity, yet at the same time I question what we sacrifice for it.

Nelson quotes Pema Chödrön that only the individual can know when "you're using things to protect yourself and keep your ego together and when you're opening and letting things fall apart, letting the world come as it is". As Nelson observes, even then you don't always know. Self-knowledge is always incomplete. Yet, much of our discourse around sexuality – and it is here that bisexuality bears the brunt – presumes that the individual is always the last to know.

Lack of knowledge and doubt are intrinsic parts of our human relationships. We can never fully know an other and, if they go, we can never fully know nor understand their reasons. Not knowing, nor understanding, the fullness of our own desires and those of others is something we have to bear. But I recognise the desperate attempts to make sense of ourselves, to make sense of our loss and pain. Ultimately, however, the only resolution is an acceptance of the pain, an acceptance of a lack of resolution.

Suddenly you were gone and your replies to me were brief. Maybe just a word. You can't row with silence. You can't make good with it either. I've learnt the trouble with asking questions of an eternal absence.

Yet I see you all around. Much more than before. I find myself talking to you. Those first nights it was in bed. I found myself rolling over to the left and realised that, while I have nothing of yours, I still have your-side-of-the-bed. Sleeping on your side of the bed is as close as I can get to holding you again.

Now I talk to you in the street. Usually you take the piss, usually you tell me to lighten up. And to show you're not being wholly cruel, you'll rest your head on my shoulder, as you used to do, and take my hand. Sometimes I'll ask you about those texts. I'll say, why did you do that? How could you leave me with that as your parting gift? But you simply smile, and turn your face so your cheek rests more comfortably on my shoulder. Because of course, it doesn't matter, does it?

The morning you left we took the overground. You had to change at Highbury and Islington, to get the bus back to Oxford, while I was to go on to the Royal Free Hospital. It was just before nine, the carriage was packed, and as we pulled in you hugged me and kissed me goodbye and even then, in that moment, with people pressing around us, trying to get out of the open doors, I worried about what people would think. And I hated myself for it, at the same time as I felt your tongue in my mouth and my face against the warm sheen of your coat. You got off the carriage and already the crowd was ahead of you, as you slowly ambled along the platform. I watched you all that time: thinking you had a slightly bow-legged gait, something of a shuffle, in your Doc Martens; and observing the chunky headphones that brushed the hair around your neck, how they hugged you like a scarf.

I feel something sad and poignant about that scene, with your backpack jumping lightly on your shoulders. I remember wanting to press the button to open the doors, to run after you, to kiss you goodbye without fear, without worrying about it. You looked so alone, isolated in emptying space. But there was my appointment at the hospital and it would be ten minutes before another train. And as we pulled out of the platform, I watched your retreating back and reckoned that would be the last time I'd ever see you. Only to dismiss it as a piece of melodrama.

But it was true. I never saw you again. That was my last sight of you. And now I'll always wish I'd run after you, down that platform.

There are those who will do anything to avoid a lack of resolution. I had a lengthy exchange with the editor of a gay magazine who claimed that anyone who sleeps with men and fails to identify as gay is doing so because of internalised homophobia. When I disagreed, he said he was not talking about those who describe themselves as bisexual or pansexual. I responded that gay was not a word that meant anything to James Baldwin, and I hope no one would accuse him of homophobia. Each of us has different, competing demands and identities.

The Pet Shop Boys' Neil Tennant had a complex relationship with his sexuality, one in which he didn't "want to belong to some narrow group or ghetto". Ramzy Alwakeel speculates that this wasn't about denial but acceptance of the many facets of Tennant's personality:

> When on a *Very* B-side [Tennant] opines that he might be "Too Many People", he isn't necessarily admitting to lying about who he is, but rather saying he genuinely might be all these contradictory identities at once.[48]

In a frantic desire for resolution, people are called out for behaviours that deviate from a social expectation as to how they should identify. The Communards singer Jimmy Somerville and critic John Gill criticised Tennant for not making his sexuality sufficiently public. However, just as Appiah observes that identity involves exclusion as well as inclusion, Eve Kosofsky Sedgwick observes in *Epistemology of the Closet* that identification "always includes multiple processes of identifying with. It also involves identification as against."[49]

This is especially true for queer people of colour and at the root of Muñoz's theory in *Disidentifications*, that those with more than one minority identity component have a particularly hard time. It often involves constant acts of identifying and counteridentifying. So, for example, a disidentification with "the normativity of whiteness in mainstream North American gay culture". This was in part the reason for Ward's focus on white men in her study, "because white men have been understood as the idealized, most normal, sort of exemplars of normal human sexuality, there's a lot of work and attention that goes into excusing anything they do."[50]

To "disidentify" is a political act that resists the dominant ideology – not through alignment with or against acts of exclusion, but by transforming them. So, there are those, like Baldwin, who believe that to identify your sexuality capitulates to a pernicious demand of the dominant ideology that pathologises sexual difference. One could even argue that, based on a particular motivation, those straight, white men in Ward's studies are disidentifying. Undoubtedly, there are reasons rooted in homophobia that mean some men do not wish to have anything to do with those they perceive as gay or homosexual. However, at the same time, there are those who have both same- and opposite-sex desire, for whom the exclusivity of terms gay and straight are negating of their experience. I may be critical of their dismissal of homosexuality as completely other. However, I recognise that our language around sexuality fails them and others. As Judith Butler observes, "It may be that the affirmation of that slippage, that the failure of identification, is itself the point of departure for a more democratizing affirmation of internal difference."[51]

Again, it comes down to an issue of the grace and dignity with which we let people speak of themselves. It means a rejection of a constant presumption of bad faith. As Nelson eloquently puts it:

How to explain, in a culture frantic for resolution, that sometimes the shit stays messy? ...How to explain that for some, or for some at some times, this irresolution is OK—desirable, even... whereas for others, or for others at some times, it stays a source of conflict or grief? How does one get across the fact that the best way to find out how people feel about their gender or their sexuality—or anything else, really—is to listen to what they tell you, and to try to treat them accordingly, without shellacking over their version of reality with yours?

Yet, just as heteronormative society places an imperative on individuals to be straight or, if in any way deviant, to own up to it and flag themselves; so, too, some gay people can enforce new imperatives. Sometimes this is the same imperative – one that demands an affinity, mistaken for solidarity – that does not make room for nuance or difference. But also, it is an increasingly invidious imperative, one that polices difference within our own community as a sign of repression – not difference – but repression.

At a symposium on identity, organised by the journal *Salmagundi*, Orlando Patterson observes that we all have multiple identities and we each may choose different aspects as the focal point.

> Where it gets problematic is when those who have
> chosen to make one aspect of their identity focal
> begin insisting that others must do no less, and
> accuse those who resist of not being sufficiently
> authentic.[52]

This goes hand-in-hand with a presumption of bad
faith. For example, the presumption that an individual
who is open about their sexuality but refuses to identify as gay or homosexual cannot be doing it for their
own, personal reasons – a refusal to accept a distortion of their experience – but can only be doing it out
of some unrealised conflict within themselves, some
internalised homophobia. Such a presumption either
makes sexuality essentialist, or presumes that the way
of being and living with our desire must be limited to
a certain set of prescribed values. These new imperatives, which shout down dissent as someone failing to
live up to a gay or queer truth, homogenise desire and
dismiss anyone with a different view or experience as
not simply different, but wrong. It creates a new imperative that demands people be "gay this way".

Such demands are a new form of oppression. When the
openly gay musician Tom Robinson married a woman
and had two children in the early nineties, there was
a backlash from some in the gay community. In 1996,
he added a verse to his famous song "Glad to be Gay"
which ran:

Well if gay liberation means freedom for all,
a label is no liberation at all.
I'm here and I'm queer and do what I do,
I'm not going to wear a straitjacket for you.

The only knowledge – understanding – I have is my own lived experience. To make universal statements from there will not work and is unfair. I can find commonality with others who are marginalised for our same-sex attraction; I can find commonality with those who also have opposite-sex attraction that conflicts with their homosexuality; I feel great commonality with those whose desires confuse and seem alien to them. But to say they are the *same*, I can't do that. I can never know. As a result, I realise that I don't know what these words mean: gay, bi, queer. Or, at least, I don't know what they mean to others. As iO Tillett Wright discovered when making *Self Evident Truths*, a photographic project documenting people in the USA who do not identify as wholly straight, there are "a million different shades of gay".[53]

When I returned my degree to Oxford University it was in part because I was learning what solidarity meant. My old college had taken a booking from a fundamentalist Christian organisation, who would go on to use the college for a conference while students were still resident, studying for their finals. Christian Concern campaign fervently against equal marriage, regard gay relationships as unnatural and immoral and support cure therapy. The Rector, Frances Cairncross, refused to apologise for the offence caused by the college's acceptance of the booking, let alone attempt to cancel it. I, and others, believed the college leadership was displaying a double standard: that were the organisation one that persecuted on grounds of race – Britain First or the Ku Klux Klan, say – the booking would have been cancelled. At the very least, I felt that the inaction of the Rector, coupled with the crassness of her replies, demonstrated a lack of concern about the rights and safety of her queer students.

You and I met for the first time the week before. It was a Sunday night and we went into that bar housed in a former chapel. We were the only customers there all evening. It was just the two of us, and the barman. You had bleached blonde hair that, coupled with a spoken intensity, gave you a white, hot glow. What was only meant to be one drink, maybe two, became however many it took until closing time. And yes, I found I loved you as early as that evening, as you yelled, "Saff! Saff!" into the great expanse where pews had once stood. And then we both began doing yoga positions on the cold, tiled floor. At one point, I arched off the ground in an approximation of a bridge pose, which I guess was an offering of some kind, or indeed a bridge to somewhere else.

Over the coming week I tried to get in touch with you, but got no reply. Eventually, I heard you'd been beaten up in Notting Hill. I couldn't believe anyone could do that to you; I wanted to ask why. But of course, I knew why. Our mutual friend told me it happened often; previously you had had your cheekbone broken.

As I considered the Rector's replies, it seemed to me that no matter what I thought – think – about nuance, it is also necessary to stand together. Particularly with those we love. That you knew it was dangerous to be you but that you did it anyway.

So when I returned my degree a week later, I didn't do it for you, but I was thinking of you when I did it.

At the same time, I have come to see that solidarity does not mean sameness. There is a difference between those with whom I express solidarity and those with whom I feel an affinity.

I also recognise there are things particular to being queer. There is a potential for intimacy opened up by queer experience and queer spaces. In his novel, Greenwell describes fleeting moments of intensity found in cruising spots. Queer experience can be democratising in the way it expands contact between people who might otherwise never meet. Goodman says of his own experience that queer promiscuity can be a beautiful thing, that "the chief human use of sex – as distinguished from the natural law of procreation – is to get to know other persons intimately."[54]

He sees the distinction between someone wanting to know us and simply know our bodies as meaningless, that sex can itself be a means of getting to know both another and ourselves.

A common criticism of homosexual promiscuity, of course, is that, rather than democracy, it involves an appalling superficiality of human conduct, so that it is a kind of archetype of the inanity of mass urban life. I doubt that this is generally the case, though I don't know; just as, of the crowds who go to art galleries, I don't know who are being spoken to by the art and who are being bewildered further—but at least some are looking for something.

Queer life has much to teach heterosexual sex. Sex can just be fun. Sexuality can be a means of getting to know someone. Promiscuity is not necessarily superficial or problematic but, like some of those in the art gallery, a demonstration of looking for something: meaning, intimacy – ultimately, a desire to be moved in our being.

Our language prioritises duration as a measure of significance. Even the definition of a relationship itself is somehow determined by how long two people have been seeing each other. But who is to define relationship? Or what counts as significant? Queer experience teaches us every instance of human desire has value. Some of my most meaningful, intense relationships have been brief, some not even physical. Value is not allied with duration. Whitman tells us this and we know it to be true.

We were never in a relationship. I can count the number of times we kissed on one hand. And that was as physically intimate as we ever became. You blew into my life with a freedom I desperately wanted for myself. You disturbed the fabric of my being. I don't know if I will even see you again, but I learnt so much from you. I remember sitting in a pub with an open fire on a cold May evening. You told me about your love of trees and we agreed that, while stars may be millennia old, there is wonder in a tree. Like the copper beech outside Tewkesbury Abbey, which stood and shaded the builders of that church, the fleeing army in the Wars of the Roses, monks and children for hundreds of years. Yet, unlike a star, we can reach out and touch it. You made things real for me. You showed life needn't only be spoken in poetry, but lived in it.

When faced with questions as to your value – messages that you matter less than your siblings, less than your cousins, less than those friends who will raise kids, that what makes you different would be better erased or hidden – you can respond in two ways. You can be intensely playful, or deeply earnest. A sense of play, a sense of taking nothing seriously, means no one can pin you down, no one can make a claim of you. All and nothing are in jest. You can also be defiant in play. You can be exactly as you want and in a manner that is both flippant and playful. A playful act of defiance is both a defence and an attack. However, at the same time, the questions that you seek answers to, the questions you internalise, take on such significance that your answers must be given in earnest, if only inside your head. Because these answers are not play, but survival.

You taught me to be playful. You told me I was sincere and earnest – and that meant people would want to take advantage and wound me. You said you were sincere but never earnest, which meant people never took you seriously, and that hurt. I resolved to take everything you did seriously, which was maybe my mistake. Of course, I also resolved to try and be more playful, which is the most fucking earnest response I could have had.

I'm troubled by a belief that there is anything intrinsic to homosexuality itself. To prescribe a range of interests, behaviours and values is a form of essentialism – sometimes predicated on exactly the loaded stereotypes that we have so long sought to avoid. Perhaps the only intrinsic experience is that all who grow up queer, as Greenwell observed, grow up in an environment where the model they are presented for normal life is not a self-image. Then again, that may change. A greater acceptance of the variety of our sexual desires and experiences may mean children growing up to parents who own and acknowledge the queer aspects of themselves – past, present and future.

I feel solidarity with fellow queer people, because social conceptions of sexuality mean that we are all other-ed. Here, solidarity is defined as a mutuality or coincidence of interests, reflecting its origins from the French *solidaire*.

I feel affinity with those with whom I have more than shared interest. Affinity is something else; affinity is a natural liking or understanding with an other. Its origins are from the Latin, quite literally meaning "to border on", from *ad-* "to" and *finis* "border". I have some ostensibly straight friends who also feel the language around sexuality to be a compromise and distortion. I feel an affinity with those who understand that, and perhaps even feel the same themselves, whether straight or gay. My affinity is with those friends with whom I share such an understanding we border each other.

I also see a commonality between those gay people who deny my bisexuality – deny my account of myself, deny the very intimate, personal matter of how I *feel* – and those straight people who police otherness in the first place. I see a commonality between all those who police and enforce sexuality, be they gay or straight, gay-bashers or deniers of bisexuality. I feel no affinity with those, gay or straight, who deny my version of myself and presume a knowledge that is not theirs to have. I see an affinity between those who erect the divide and police it with intensity, regardless of which side of it they stand on.

So, I feel solidarity with other queer people, but an affinity only with those who take how I feel as the last word on my own feelings; just as I feel affinity with those straight people who have no interest in policing the divide, because they know – either through me or their own experience – both how porous and also, ultimately, how inhuman such a division truly is.

Above and beyond this, I see my solidarity with those on both sides of this artificial dividing line. I see their commonality with each other, my commonality with them; that we are all, first and foremost, people.

I worry over an increasing dynamic on the left, and amongst some gay people, in which a divergence of views can be dismissed on grounds of perceived prejudice or lack of radicalism. For example, when queer people express solidarity but are *still* rejected for not identifying or behaving in the "right" way, as happened to Tennant and Robinson. Such a rejection of others is intolerance, a lack of solidarity. Why should my sexuality mean or imply anything about me other than who I am attracted to? As much as I am sceptical about gay Tories or Republicans, on the grounds that they fail to interrogate other forms of oppression similar to our own, I cannot accept essentialism that mandates a particular politics. Just as I cannot accept the kind of essentialism that suggests all gay men like flowers, musicals or watching Eurovision; or that gay women have short hair, play women's rugby and like to settle down.

During a night out at the theatre with a group of friends, someone suggested a club we could all go to another evening. It was pointed out that a guy who had failed to join our party wouldn't like it, and so began a long discussion of this as symptomatic of his repression, his internalised homophobia. I interjected that he didn't like many clubs and, by the sound of it, this wasn't a place I'd like much either. But increasingly I fear that the scepticism bisexual men and women live with is permeating other parts of queer life and leftist politics. We forget that we can show solidarity without all being the same.

I fear this demonstrates a continuing lack of confidence in ourselves. A solidarity that silences difference with a dismissal of "internalised homophobia" is not comfortable with variety and dissent in its own ranks. Yet, as with the scepticism of bisexuals, the hyperconscious "critique" only ever goes one way. Those interrogating the subtle motivations of our absent friend that night did not also reflect upon whether their need for him to share all their tastes suggested an insecurity in their own sexuality, which meant they only felt comfortable with those who shared all their own preferences. It seems the mirror is only ever to be held up to others, never to be looked into.

Why do we need the mirror at all?

There is something similarly simplistic in the trajectory that queries those who "come out" for a reluctance to embrace their new, public commonality with those who share their sexual orientation. Having witnessed this very moment in friends and lovers, it does not seem to me that this is always a lack of resolution with oneself – *it can be precisely the opposite*. If those you love, those you are closest to, those with whom you share your history, your interests, do not share your sexual desire, the issue is how to understand this aspect of yourself *without* abandoning the people and things that *you* feel make you yourself. In other words, we are more than simply the sex of those we desire; indeed, we may have more in common – a greater affinity – with those people who *do not* share our sexual orientation. That does not mean all those for whom that is the case are repressed or in denial; it is simply their complex resolution of all the aspects of themselves that make them who they are.

This does not seem to me a controversial observation.

UK magazine *Gay Times* got grief for running a blog post by Gary Keery, a gay man brought up in 1980s Northern Ireland, expressing his own lingering homophobia. The response online was almost universal condemnation, ranging from "This is so fucking awful I can't believe this exists", to "Behold: an utter wanker". However, the writer wasn't advocating the homophobic views he had internalised, he was simply recounting his experience. A solidarity that silences its members from expressing their own problems does not seem to me a solidarity worth having. Setting aside the lack of compassion for someone whose own experience of their sexuality has left them with conflicting feelings, including shame, many of the replies also demand that sexuality comes with a series of preconceived, universal values and ideas. Those who deviate from these norms are accused of internal homophobia. But as drag queen Panti Bliss told an audience at Dublin's Abbey Theatre, we are all homophobic.

> I do, it is true, believe that almost all of you are probably homophobes. But I'm a homophobe. It would be incredible if we weren't. To grow up in a society that is overwhelmingly and stiflingly homophobic and to somehow escape unscathed would be miraculous.[55]

All of us will be victims, to some degree, of our own internalised homophobia. What matters is whether we can acknowledge and accept that in ourselves and others with grace, or whether we wish to silence. An accusation of "internalised homophobia" is not only a brilliant way to silence a fellow queer person, it is also an act of arrogance. It states that we have no internalised homophobia, yet we can always recognise it when we see it in others. It also acts as an instruction to others to ignore the accused. It says: this person is not worth listening to.

Like Ward's observation that Cynthia Nixon was told off for daring to tell the American people that sexuality is fluid, Keery was condemned for daring to articulate the feelings of fear and shame that queer people must contend with and overcome. For some, silencing those voices is easier than the pain or memories of it. However, psychoanalysis tells us how disastrous such a root can be. Muñoz evolves the work of Kosofsky Sedgwick, who observed that rather than being "toxic" parts of an individual or group identity, the forms taken by shame are integral to identity and residual to its formation. Rather than dispelling contradictory elements, he argues, "a disidentifying subject works to hold on to this object and invest it with new life". We cannot pick and choose our reality; instead we must inhabit and make our own the totality of our experience.

The language around a common homosexual identity results in new forms of scepticism. The hurtful division between straight and gay results in new binaries: universalism and particularity, assimilation and radicalism, normative and transgressive.

This is a continuation of the scepticism suffered by

bisexuals. We treat with suspicion those who deviate from our own view, while always treating our own position as an uncomplicated, unquestionable truth. There's something deeply illiberal about a growing social trend that wants to call out others and presupposes bad faith. Labels are used as a means of dismissing, not engaging with, others: Blairite, Corbynista, red Tory, Bernie Bros, Remoaner, Libtard. All of these are indicators of the other side's presumed bad faith and a virtuous signal of our ability to see them for what they are.

Yet, all of us have our own compromises to make, our own negotiation between the version of ourselves that makes political sense and our complex, lived reality. Like Nelson, I can understand those who are anxious their allies should speak clearly and in terms like their own. Yet, as she observes, *"People are different from each other.* Unfortunately, the dynamic of becoming a spokesperson almost always threatens to bury this fact."* However, that should never trump the personal imperative of our own truth. No account of ourselves is truthful if it is compromised and distorted.

At the *Salmagundi* symposium on identity, Robert Boyers defended Lionel Trilling. Trilling was condemned by some for being insufficiently Jewish, or in flight from his Jewishness. Boyers, who knew him, asked: "Do people who are Jewish look Jewish? ...Are they supposed to look Jewish just to satisfy Alfred Kazin or Sidney Morgenbesser that they aren't hiding something?" He went on to say that Trilling was exactly what he appeared – a complex man who, if he had appeared ethnically self-conscious, as others demanded, would have been doing so out of pretence. In his own way, Trilling was true to himself, "a man with many conflicts and ambivalences".

The sometime vehemence of my rejection of a blanket queer affinity might be mistaken for an underlying desire to assimilate. But I don't believe it is that, so much as a rejection of a kind of queer group behaviour, which Goodman cautions against. Describing a certain kind of spite – "the vitality of the powerless" – he identifies one sort as the "in-group fanatic, feeling that only his own kind are authentic and have soul". He warns that this is self-disproving, like trying to prove you have a sense of humour. There is a difference yet similarity between the reactionaries, who deny any affinity with their fellow queer people, and the in-group fanatics who deny affinity with anyone but.

Similarly, Appiah cautions against ghettoisation, when he warns those who identify as gay to not only talk to one another. He says that regardless of colour, culture, creed and country, those whom we have affinity with are not necessarily those who share what we regard as our identity. Identity is amorphous. Identity is not deterministic. Above all, I take this as a reminder that our chief solidarity is our shared humanity.

When Goodman describes his experience as an outsider inspiring him "to want a more elementary humanity, wilder, less structured, more variegated, and where people pay attention to one another", he gives voice to my own hope. He speaks to me of a difference of solidarity between the universal and particular – a solidarity with our fellow oppressed, whomever they are, but a recognition of our common humanity. A more "elementary humanity" echoes Baldwin; while "less structure" is a disavowal of our categorisation and compartmentalising, instead choosing to see our shared variety. Above all, it pays attention to each of us for our individual selves.

When Bindel says, "Tolerance is one thing, acceptance is slightly better, but assimilation is a defeat for gay and straight alike", it presumes that we all know what assimilation means; that we are all agreed on what the "norm" is, what the values are, that are being assimilated. It also presumes that the very fact of something being the norm means it must be negative. It means our outsider status places a political imperative upon us to disown some of the things we may want.

We cannot live outside our context. We cannot divorce from our past. We cannot unmake ourselves. Psychoanalysis shows we must first come to terms with who we are; paradoxically, change is only possible by first forgetting about change in the face of this brute fact. In Damon Galgut's *The Beautiful Screaming of Pigs*, the narrator reflects on his own courage, or lack of it. A freedom fighter, whom he admired, has been killed, and he sits with the man's widow, reflecting on all that he cannot be:

There were other words behind these ones, a confession straining to be made, but it couldn't come out. If I could have spoken I might have said something like this: *your lover who died was all that I'll never be. Though I strain and I beat, my efforts are muffled, my cries are eaten by silence. Andrew Lovell was my other impossible self.*[56]

Psychoanalysis teaches us that we can only be as brave as we are and that the first act of bravery is accepting the fact of ourselves. Part of the narrator's plight is his inability to be himself. By refusing to accept himself as he is, he denies the opportunity for change. He is unable to utter the words he wants to speak, unable to turn back and look at the woman. Paradoxically, our desire to be other than we are can be what stops our mouths, stops our feet, from voicing and enacting the change we wish to see.

There is still that part of me that wants to satisfy the small boy who grew up in a small town, conservative, Church of England family, where what you did was get married. I don't want it *for* that per se, but because those are the lives chosen and lived by some whom I love. It is not for me to dismiss them as insufficiently radical. I recognise a goodness of its own, in that dream.

David Steiner told the identity symposium about General Robert E. Lee who was invited to be general of both the North and South armies during the American Civil War. Steiner recounts that Lee genuinely agonised over the decision and recognised that, ethically, "the North was probably the preferable side to pick, though like Socrates in the *Crito* he ended up saying I cannot be other than I am." That was: a man from Virginia, a man of the South. Steiner recounts how stupid – "risible" – his students found this decision, but asks whether the idea that the more educated we are the greater our ability to perceive our own false consciousness, or bad faith, is mere hubris.

> Do we really deep down believe that the more educated we are, the more we're released from the claims of the given, or is it conceivable that in fact that's a double hubris, and the deeper fantasy is the fantasy of release?

If Foucault showed us anything, it is the futility of imagining ourselves able to step outside systems. I cannot unmake myself. I cannot remake myself with a different background or a different past. I can question the assumptions and values of it, but I cannot erase the people who made me, the context that has created me. That *is* my past. It always will be. My goal here is simply freedom. I believe that to be radical.

When I interviewed Greenwell for *The White Review,* I observed that his novel succeeds in holding in tension the particularity of queer experience, the fleeting moments of intimacy, the possibility of a different experience, while also acknowledging the painful exclusion that confronts queer people. "A measure of the world's beneficence" is withheld from us, and sometimes the result is that voiced in Mitko's moving, exhausted line:

"I want to lead a normal life." This tension – between radicalism and assimilation, particularity and universalism – is an internal tension within all queer people, he observes.

> That schism has existed in the LGBT movement from the very beginning, from that aspect of the movement that says, "We are the same as you, love is love, we're not different at all." And that version that says, "No we're quite different from you and we have distinct models of life and community and expression that are valuable in and of themselves." Those two differences, between a desire to assimilate and a desire to assert a radical difference, are also a schism within many queer people. That is the kind of contrary energy that can be very productive when it comes to works of art, and when it comes to life as a work of art. In politics it is much harder to sustain.[57]

I don't believe we can be reconciled to our own, inherent contradictions as long as we speak of ourselves like political actors. Political expediency requires a denial of them. Yet the contradictions that exist within us, as with all people, cannot be resolved but simply held. To deny them is also a compromise, a distortion of who we really are.

I understand the anxiety around equal marriage. I understand Greenwell's welcoming of marriage equality, while at the same time his wondering about the assimilation of queer people into a system that used to oppress us, and still does. I recognise and hate the institutional misogyny of marriage and the very fact that marriage *is* an institution. The radicalism that has become mine, as a result of my difference, means I hate and mistrust the shallow commercialism by which marriage is sold as the ideal.

Yet I cannot deny that on some profound level the idea of marriage is deeply meaningful to me. And this demonstrates to me that my reason, my politics, only cut so deep.

Marriage holds a force for me as a sacrament. I say this without denomination, without a religious conviction; yet at the same time I feel my world shaped by belief. That some things have a profundity, a depth, that remains at the same time strange to us seems to me undeniable. For me, marriage has the potential to transcend the politics and cultural misogyny that have so badly damaged it. Marriage as sacrament holds a force. Marriage as sacrament, in all of the definitions given by the dictionary, is something that I want: "an oath, a solemn engagement; esp. one confirmed by ritual", "a thing of sacred character or significance", "a mystery", "a type or symbol *of* something", "a religious ceremony or act regarded as imparting spiritual grace to the participants".

I am persuaded by the idea of an act, a ritualistic act, that has a significance that remains mysterious to me. Whenever I enter a church or chapel, I light a candle for my father. I do not believe in an afterlife, a heaven, in any conventional sense. But the idea of a votive candle, the smoke from which carries our prayers to God and, in this case, our love and thoughts to those we've lost, ultimately a gesture that speaks of something beyond us, touches me deeply, on a profound level beyond my reason.

So, I understand the arguments against marriage; I sympathise, even agree with, the rejection of marriage as an institution. But I cannot lose the idea of marriage as a sacrament, for it touches me somewhere beyond my sight and understanding.

Similarly, it was for this reason that I hoped you'd accompany me to the Midnight Mass at Tewkesbury Abbey, for no better reason than it seemed the place we'd most likely find my Dad. This is odd, as the Midnight was pretty much the only service at the Abbey I never knew him go to. But as he dedicated his life to the building, as his choir sings there each weekday evening, as his resting place is marked by a square of turf and a rose in the garden of remembrance, I feel that is where he might be found. And in some ways, I suppose it is where I am to be found too. In the building where my parents married, where my sister married; the building where we went for prayers each morning in term time. I wanted to show you that, and for you to see it.

But you didn't. And now you are no longer here, I can never show it to you. You were never destined to meet my father even in that mad, irrational way of mine. Now I light a candle, one for each of you: one for you, and one for him. There are moments, all too brief, where the pair of you stand side by side, lighting the dark. Such actions have a resonance.

In my discussion with Greenwell, I struggled with the division between politics and art. Of course, I can understand it, the expediency, the necessity for us to speak the language of politics. To fight for our rights requires that of us. "The certainty with which one has to speak in the political realm of activism is the opposite of the realm of art, which is the realm of ambivalence and uncertainty and doubt." Yet, such a demand means we speak of ourselves with a simplicity that is the opposite of being human. None of us should have to concede our complexity as the condition for our equality. To be treated equally means not having to make that concession. We must live with the tensions that exist in us all. They are part of what makes us human, as opposed to a machine or political slogan. They are our humanity. They are the stuff of art.

I recognise how maddening this must be. I agree with Goodman that a writer may be a decent citizen in a perfect community, "but he is an unreliable ally – he is 'unrealistic' – in actual politics". Yet I make no apology for this. In respect of queer lives, art has a political function, which is to remind us of how much we have lost, how much we have had to give up in terms of how we talk about and see ourselves. The political imperative on queer people to identify, to be a spokesperson, erases nuance, difference and the individual subjectivity of our lived experience.

Nelson gets this when she argues it is unsustainable to demand that any of us can live a life that is simply one thing. This means that all of us will, in our different ways, assimilate and transgress, be both radical yet normative. The kind of exceptionalism that rejects bisexual people as not different enough, or mandates that solidarity must come with toeing a particular line, mistakes solidarity for an erasure of any difference. It is the consequence of political language infecting our being, the consequence of an oppression that leaves us too insecure to feel comfortable with difference.

> Think of how freaked some people got when activist/actress Cynthia Nixon described her experience of her sexuality as "a choice". But while *I can't change even if I tried* may be a true and moving anthem for some, it's a piss-poor one for others. At a certain point the tent may need to give way to field.

Decisions aren't made on the basis of courage or radicalism alone. Or sometimes at all. They are made on the basis of who we are, whom we desire and, above all, what is possible for us.

For me, it is about a person and what feels right. What we both want. No one should be held to an ideal set by others in relation to love. Mine with one woman is different to mine with another, or with a man, or another man. My love is not yours; yours is not mine.

As Nelson observes, revolutionary language can become a sort of fetish. "Perhaps it's the word *radical* that needs rethinking. But what could we angle ourselves toward instead, or in addition? Openness? Is that good enough, strong enough?" And I don't know. But I know where I've come from and I know there's nothing I can do about that. I also know whom I've loved and that those individuals – whom I've loved for themselves, not their sex – is where I want to go. In those moments I'm not concerned with either the assimilation into "normal" society, nor making a radical stand. I'm in love. It strikes me that *that* is the ideal. I say so without denying that to reach it and desire it is political. But the loving is not. Baldwin was right.

What I want in those moments is for nothing but that to matter. That is when it ceases to be political but purely personal. That is when I am free.

I sometimes wonder whether this book is my way of never having to talk about sexuality again. Like so much else, it is a response that denies the need for a response. This is it, I want to say. After years in which my sexuality was a topic of negotiation, now I see that there is no negotiation, no discussion.

I fear that my differences with some gay friends are indivisible. And not because one of us is right or wrong, or because we've not tried sufficiently to understand or appreciate the other's view, but because this is the kind of thing that cannot be agreed. That identity, like religious faith, is a kind of belief: like religious faith, we may share some of the same tenets but the nuance of what we believe, the way we live and walk in our faith, is different. And that can only ever be so. The error, with identity as well as faith, is to see these differences of perspective, of experience, as symptomatic of unbelief or apostasy.

It is the difference between solidarity and affinity; the difference between mutual interest and a relationship that is so close we border on each other.

It is also an acceptance of my inability to fully know; an acknowledgement that my desire will always remain a mystery to me and that, therefore, how much more unknowable to me must be the desires of others. Phillips argues that we cannot know people as desiring creatures, that in terms of accepting people as sexual, "knowing them in any conscious way may not be the best, the most promising, thing we can do with them." Of the things we can know of others, all it really reveals is how little we know; "how little knowing can do for us".

This process of writing has revealed that the only certainty I can assert is my paradoxical certainty in doubt. As Phillips observes of individuals, "when it comes to love what is revealed is that one desires but one has no idea what it is that one desires." The same can be said of sexuality. Sexuality is about more than simply who we have sex with. Given that how, what and why we desire all remain mysterious to us, then the notion that our desire, our sexuality, is simply about the sex of those we sleep with is facile.

Our contemporary language of sexuality categorizes and pathologizes something that can never fully be known. It is not the kind of thing that can be known. At the same time, this language disenfranchises the vast numbers of men and women for whom the terms "heterosexual" and "homosexual" are not exclusive but in synchrony.

We must be inventive with language rather than defined by it; we need to find the words that create us anew in each act of love.

The hegemony of scientific materialism does not adequately express our experiential reality. As Goodman observes, "Specialist science and its value-neutral language are an avoidance of experience, a narrow limitation of the self, and an act of bad faith."[58] We know that the world we experience is more complex and mysterious than the descriptions and language given to us by positivism and empiricism.

A recent exhibition of Paul Nash's work at the Tate featured an undated typescript titled "Dreams". Nearby were his depictions of the spring equinox and summer solstice, images that feature both the sun and the moon, each present in the same sky. Nash writes:

> The divisions we may hold between night and day – waking world and that of the dream, reality and the other thing, do not hold. They are penetrable, they are porous, translucent, transparent; in a word they are not there.

Similarly, I know that the divisions between heterosexual and homosexual, masculine and feminine, are artificial. They too are penetrable, porous, translucent and transparent. That is my experiential certainty. The categorisation and commodification of desire results in a poverty of experience.

In defending literary language against the forces of positivism, Goodman invokes Percy Bysshe Shelley and his *Defence of Poetry* as the only thing that can liberate and bring together our fragmented world, a world in which we *know* through the imaginative faculty more than our science can tell us:

> Poetry enlarges the circumference of the imagination…We want the creative faculty to imagine that which we know: our calculations have outrun conception…The cultivation of those sciences which have enlarged the limits of the empire of man over the external world has, for want of the poetical faculty, proportionately circumscribed those of the internal world.[59]

Art's power lies in its paradoxical relationship with truth. As Greenwell observed, "There is a kind of special power or efficacy in fiction and in imaginative art precisely because it so staunchly and uncompromisingly defends itself from the claims of truth." Yet, at the same time, it is this freedom – freedom from assertion, freedom from argument – that allows art to make claims of its own. As Goodman argues, these claims are not, and can never be, the truth claims of science:

How do these traits and powers of literary writing add up to a warrant to make true statements, in the sense that scientific statements are true? They don't. *But there is no alternative.* There is no other discourse but literature that is subjective and objective, general and concrete, spontaneous and deliberate, and that, though it is just thinking aloud, gives so much attention to language, our chief communication. [His italics.]

Writers are not committed "to find confirmable and replicable truth", Goodman observes. Like Nestor in the *Iliad*, artists work to make sense of our experience, our being: at no stage did Nestor dissuade the Greeks, but Goodman argues, "it was no doubt a good thing for them to go to their doom with open eyes."

Negative capability requires a stepping back, a withdrawal from assertion, an acceptance of limited understanding. It is an acceptance of our not knowing. At the same time, it is also a paradoxical act of faith. For it both accepts a half-knowledge, while believing in the potential for a fuller understanding that transcends those limits by our acceptance of that very same uncertainty, limitation and doubt. As Paul Ricœur observed when arguing for a synthesis of interpretation, the contrary of suspicion is faith:

No longer, to be sure, the first faith of the simple soul, but rather the second faith of one who has engaged in hermeneutics, faith that has undergone criticism, postcritical faith... It is a rational faith, for it interprets; but it is a faith because it seeks, through interpretation, a second naïveté... "Believe in order to understand, understand in order to believe" — such is its maxim.[60]

On expanding the point, Ricœur argues that "the mytho-poetic core of imagination" is at stake.

Nelson describes Anne Carson giving a lecture in which she introduced her to "the concept of leaving a space empty so that God could rush in". This is an acceptance of our negative capability, the limits of our ability to know. It is an acceptance akin to Coetzee's notion of grace. An acknowledgement of reason's limitations – a withdrawal from the false promise of a hyperconscious rationalism – leaves room for doubt, uncertainties, but one with creative potential. This potential is for an intuition beyond reason, a space empty for what Ricœur calls the "grace of imagination, the upsurge of the possible".

Coetzee expresses his sympathy with those whose thinking is "disordered". He speculates that "People rarely – in fact almost never – act on the basis of reason: people act on the basis of impulse or desire or urge or drive or passion or mood, and dress up their motives afterwards to make them seem reasonable."[61] Whether or not we agree with him, what is undeniable is that desire itself is not part of the reasonable, rational realm. That is part of its particularity. And for that reason, again, I come back to the sense that universal proclamations about our desire, our sexualities, as though these things have a common frame, are meaningless. To attempt to codify and delimit desire is to deny its very nature. This observation has the greatest force for those in some way bisexual, whose way of thinking about our desire – our way of speaking with the language available to us – can only ever be disordered.

The imperative placed on queer people to account for ourselves is a discriminatory act that demeans our human dignity. It is not a demand made of heterosexuals: they do not need to account for themselves; their desire does not need to be reduced to the language of politics, of stance. As Greenwell told me, "Art is the realm in which contradictions can be held and not resolved, but held in a kind of beneficent stasis." That is like sexuality, desire like art: a creative act that reveals something of us anew in each act of desiring. Anything less is a compromise, a distortion of ourselves and the rights we should be afforded. I will not accept that the heteronormative may love in the language of art, but I may only love in the language of politics. So, at one and the same time, my refusal to answer is a recognition of the unknowable nature of sexuality, and a paradoxical political stance that rejects the imperative to be political. As Nelson said of a friend, "How can I tell her that *not trying* has become the whole point, the whole plan?"

The French original of Christine and the Queens' song "Tilted" named "Christine" uses 'do not care to' in relation to 'debout', or 'stand up'. I understand this as both literal – "I cannot stand up" physically, in the manner of standing and identifying with others – but also the contextual meaning in French of an argument standing up to scrutiny. Far more subtle than the notion of "tilted", the song asks us to see "Christine" as she is: a complex and not necessarily coherent being. After all, such is the nature of being human. The stance is at one and the same time political, while rejecting the notion of individual as a coherent political stance. Above all, we are asked to see her common humanity as one with us all, for whom "the sky passes over our hands".

I do not stand up. My sexuality – the way I *feel*, the way I inhabit myself and the values I espouse do not cohere. They do not form a neat politics, a tract. But then why should they? This is not something demanded of every-body – it is only demanded of those of us in some way othered. But, *the world also belongs to me*.

This is what happened. I was midway through the pitch for this book when I got the call with the news you'd died. When I hung up I thought that was it – there was no way I could think about nor write this now. And then I realised I had to – because no one had inspired me more or taught me as much about having the courage to live as you did, yourself. I owed you that. And more. So I tried to write but I found myself writing to you. I'd lost you long before, but, in losing you again, I found you, because in the act of writing I had you in mind. As I began to write I found myself addressing you. And not just you, but others too. Once I started I couldn't stop and gradually it dawned on me that this could only ever have been the way to say what I needed to say – personally and subjectively. And I realised that, of course, I couldn't write this without thinking of you, because the only way I know any of these things is through you. All of you.

Notes

1. https://www.youtube.com/watch?v=IWRuQ8C-JOFg

2. https://www.youtube.com/watch?v=OJw-JnoB9EKw

3. https://www.theguardian.com/commentis-free/2013/dec/02/tom-daley-bisexual-sexuali-ty-diver-relationship-man

4. Milaine Alarie and Stéphanie Gaudet, "'I Don't Know If She Is Bisexual or If She Just Wants to Get Attention': Analyzing the Various Mechanisms Through Which Emerging Adults Invisibilize Bisexuality", *Journal of Bisexuality*, Volume 13, Issue 2 (Taylor & Francis Group, 2013).

5. Maggie Nelson, *The Argonauts* (Melville House UK, 2015).

6. http://www.dailystar.co.uk/showbiz/372743/Tom-Daley-reveals-he-is-gay-not-bisexual-on-Celebri-ty-Juice

7. http://www.pinknews.co.uk/2014/04/03/tom-da-ley-im-definitely-gay-not-bisexual

8. https://www.theguardian.com/sport/2015/jul/18/tom-daley-i-always-knew-i-was-attracted-to-guys-olympic-2012-diver

9. "The Last Interview" by Quincy Troupe, *James Baldwin: The Last Interview and Other Conversations* (Melville House Publishing, 2014).

10. http://www.bbc.co.uk/programmes/po4bnkc6

11. https://www.youtube.com/watch?v=pa1Ux67rD1Q

12. Ian Thorpe, *This is Me: The Autobiography* (Simon & Schuster, 2013).

13. "The Queer Apologetic: Explaining the Use of Bisexuality as a Transitional Identity", Nicholas Guittar, Journal of Bisexuality, Volume 13, Issue 2 (Taylor & Francis Group, 2013).

14. https://www.theguardian.com/commentis-free/2014/apr/20/alan-carr-gay-men-homophobia-camp-prejudice

15. http://www.gq-magazine.co.uk/article/george-mi-chael-interview

16. Michel Foucault, *The Will to Knowledge: The History of Sexuality Volume 1* (Penguin Books, 1998).

17. Adam Phillips, *Missing Out: In Praise of the Unlived Life* (Penguin Books, 2013).

18. Lisa Diamond, *Sexual Fluidity: Understanding Women's Love and Desire* (Cambridge, Mass.: Harvard University Press, 2009).

19. Greta R. Bauer and David J. Brennan, "The Problem with 'Behavioral Bisexuality': As-sessing Sexual Orientation in Survey Research", *Journal of Bisexuality*, Volume 13, Issue 2 (Taylor & Francis Group, 2013).

20. https://www.ons.gov.uk/peoplepopulationand-community/culturalidentity/sexuality/bulletins/sexualidentityuk/2015

21. https://yougov.co.uk/news/2015/08/16/half-young-not-heterosexual/

22. David Halperin, *One Hundred Years of Homosexual-ity: And Other Essays on Greek Love* (New York: Rou-tledge, 1990).

23. Michael Rocke, *Forbidden Friendships: Homosexual-ity and Male Culture in Renaissance Florence* (Oxford: Oxford University Press, 1996).

24. Joe Moran, *Shrinking Violets: A Field Guide to Shyness* (London: Profile Books, 2016).

25. Robert Aldrich, *Gay Lives* (New York: Thames & Hudson, 2012).

26. http://www.thewhitereview.org/interviews/interview-garth-greenwell/

27. Marjorie Garber, *Bisexuality and the Eroticism of Everyday Life* (New York: Routledge, 2000).

28. https://www.youtube.com/watch?v=IWRuQ8C-JOFg

29. Anana Schofield, "The Difficult Question", *Alchemy: Writers of Truth, Lies and Fiction* (Notting Hill Editions Ltd, 2016).

30. Milaine Alarie and Stéphanie Gaudet, "'I Don't Know If She Is Bisexual or If Just Wants to Get Attention': Analysing the Various Mechanisms Through Which Emerging Adults Invisibilize Bisexuality", *Journal of Bisexuality*, Volume 13, Issue 2 (Taylor & Francis Group, 2013).

31. https://www.theguardian.com/society/2016/dec/03/being-bisexual-ruby-tandoh-comment-st-vincent-cara-delevingne

32. Dennis Altman, Homosexual: *oppression and liberation* (London: Allen Lane, 1974).

33. James Baldwin, *Giovanni's Room* (London: Penguin, 2000).

34. Julie Bindel, *Straight Expectations: What Does It Mean to Be Gay Today?* (London: Guardian Books, 2014).

35. Garth Greenwell, *What Belongs to You* (New York: Farrar, Straus and Giroux, 2016).

36. John Donne, *The Major Works*, edited by John Carey (Oxford: Oxford University Press, 2000).

37. Christopher Isherwood, *A Single Man* (London: Vintage Books, 2000).
38. Rita Felski, *The Limits of Critique* (Chicago: University of Chicago Press, 2015).
39. J. M. Coetzee, *Doubling the Point* (Cambridge, Mass.: Harvard University Press, 1992).
40. Simon Critchley, *Notes on Suicide* (London: Fitzcarraldo Editions, 2016).
41. Gary Gutting, *Foucault: A Very Short Introduction* (New York: Oxford University Press, 2005).
42. https://youtu.be/OfEyzsEwlGE
43. https://www.stonewall.org.uk/sites/default/files/Mental_Health_Stonewall_Health_Briefing__2012_.pdf
44. John Keats, *The Major Works*, edited by Elizabeth Cook (Oxford: Oxford University Press, 2001).
45. Maggie Nelson, *Bluets* (Wave Books, 2009).
46. Walt Whitman, *The Complete Poems of Walt Whitman* (Wordsworth Editions Ltd, 2006).
47. José Esteban Muñoz, *Disidentifications: Queers of Color and the Performance of Politics* (Minneapolis: University of Minnesota Press, 1999).
48. Ramzy Alwakeel, *Smile If You Dare: Pointy Hats and Politics with the Pet Shop Boys, 1993-1994* (London: Repeater Books, 2016).
49. Eve Kosofsky Sedgwick, *Epistemology of the Closet* (Berkeley, Calif.: University of California Press, 2008).
50. http://nymag.com/scienceofus/2015/08/why-straight-men-have-sex-with-each-other.html
51. Judith Butler, *Bodies that Matter* (New York: Routledge, 1993).

52. "Identity: A Salmagundi Symposium", *Salmagundi*, Issues 192–3 (New York: Skidmore College, 2010).

53. http://www.ted.com/talks/io_tillett_wright_fifty_ shades_of_gay?utm_source=tedcomshare&utm_ medium=referral&utm_campaign=tedspread

54. http://www.selfevidentproject.com

55. Paul Goodman, *Crazy Hope and Finite Experience: final essays of Paul Goodman*, ed. Taylor Stoehr (San Francisco: Jossey-Bass, 1994).

56. Damon Galgut, *The Beautiful Screaming of Pigs* (London: Atlantic Books, 2006).

57. http://www.thewhitereview.org/interviews/inter-view-garth-greenwell/

58. Paul Goodman, *Speaking and Language: Defence of Poetry* (New York: Random House, 1972).

59. Percy Bysshe Shelley, *Selected Poems and Prose* (London: Penguin Books, 2016).

60. Paul Ricœur, *Freud and Philosophy: An Essay on Inter-pretation* (New Haven: Yale University Press, 1970).

61. J. M. Coetzee and Arabella Kurtz, "'Nevertheless, My Sympathies are with the Karamazovs': A Cor-respondence", *Salmagundi*, Volume 10, Issues 166–7 (New York: Skidmore College, 2010).

Acknowledgements

I am immensely grateful to the following people for making this book possible. Tom Overton and the editors of *The White Review*, Jacques Testard and Ben Eastham, who encouraged me to pursue this project and advised me how to proceed. They are each inspirations in their own right. Tariq Goddard, Josh Turner and the team at Repeater Books for believing in me and the value of this as a book; my agent Karolina Sutton for her patience, support and encouragement over the years; Garth Greenwell for meeting with me and agreeing to be interviewed – the subtleties and nuance he expressed helped me find a way through my own experience. Arts Council England provided a grant, without which I could not have written this book. I am eternally grateful to them and Gemma Seltzer and Charlotte Aston for their advice. My supervisors at Birkbeck, Toby Litt and Peter Fifield, not only encouraged me when I should have been studying but have also inspired me, helped me and led me to whole new avenues of research, reading and ways to write.

Many friends have loved and supported me in the inception and writing of this book. Too many to name here. They have read drafts, engaged in lengthy discussions and listened to me from the start. You know who you are and, for the avoidance of doubt, I shall tell you and thank you again.

Thanks to Ciara Mulvenna for the French translation. Also to Carlos Fishman for listening; Tom Dillon for being my first reader; Rudy Katoch for introducing me to *Disidentifications*; Miquel Bibiloni Pons for proving

Paul Goodman right; Jo Humphreys for her friendship and being my wife from another life; Doug Brennan for reminding me of what matters; and Jeri Johnson for instilling the confidence in me and so many others to be ourselves.

Finally, I want to pay special thanks to Alfie Stroud and Rudolph Slobins: Alfie for his love and friendship, for listening, for agreeing and disagreeing, for always acting with grace – our discussions have shaped my own understanding and so much of what is here; Rudolph for simply being himself, with his example of indifference and defiance that were, and are, an inspiration. I continue to miss him.

Supported using public funding by

LOTTERY FUNDED

ARTS COUNCIL ENGLAND

Repeater Books

Repeater Books is dedicated to the creation of a new reality. The landscape of twenty-first-century arts and letters is faded and inert, riven by fashionable cynicism, egotistical self-reference and a nostalgia for the recent past. Repeater intends to add its voice to those movements that wish to enter history and assert control over its currents, gathering together scattered and isolated voices with those who have already called for an escape from Capitalist Realism. Our desire is to publish in every sphere and genre, combining vigorous dissent and a pragmatic willingness to succeed where messianic abstraction and quiescent co-option have stalled: abstention is not an option: we are alive and we don't agree.

Repeater

#0106 - 160718 - C0 - 197/125/8 - PB - 9781910924716